MEET THE SUPERSTARS

WALTON: "I feel that the place of sports in society should be as a means of drawing people from different backgrounds closer together, a means of having fun, and a means of promoting better health . . . for the masses, not just for a few."

THOMPSON: "I try to give the fans their money's worth every night. But don't forget, we have so many good players that I can be terrible and we still win. So it doesn't get me down if I don't have a real good night, because I know I can come back the next night. You have to take those things in stride in pro basketball."

LANIER: "I take Jabbar outside and try to drive the hoop more than I do against other teams. That's something I couldn't do when I first came into the league. In fact, my second year he had a mental thing over me. He *knew* he could beat me. But he doesn't know that anymore."

COLLINS: "We talk of sacrifice and common goals, but when it comes time to do it, we stand around. When we need a big basket or key play, we fall apart. This team can't just push a talent button and get away with it. We're always going to be semi-disorganized. Yeah, I'm skeptical of how good we really are."

Superstars

Walton ★ Thompson
Lanier ★ Collins

by Bill Gutman

tempo books

GROSSET & DUNLAP
A FILMWAYS COMPANY
Publishers • New York

**To my good friends
Jan and Tony Pickett**

Copyright © 1977 by Bill Gutman
All rights reserved
ISBN: 0-448-14544-8
A Tempo Books Original
Tempo Books is registered in the U.S. Patent Office
Published simultaneously in Canada
Printed in the United States of America

ACKNOWLEDGMENTS

The author would like to thank the sports information departments at St. Bonaventure University, Illinois State University, North Carolina State University, and UCLA, as well as the publicity departments of the Detroit Pistons, Philadelphia 76ers, Denver Nuggets, and Portland Trail Blazers for helping furnish background information used in preparation of this book. A special thanks to the National Basketball Association's public relations department for their usual thorough and prompt response to requests for help.

CONTENTS

Bill Walton	1
David Thompson	54
Bob Lanier	97
Doug Collins	136
Statistics	183

★ BILL WALTON ★

★ At the end of the 1976-77 basketball season, NBA fans had a new hero. He was Bill Walton, the center for the world champion Portland Trail Blazers. Walton not only had a great season; he also triggered the Blazers to victory over four very tough opponents in the playoffs. And when those playoffs ended the Trail Blazers had proved once more that there's no substitute for good team basketball.

It was a special season for Bill Walton in many ways. He was with a winning team once more—better yet a champion team. And he had finally proved that he was one of the best centers not only of this day, but of any day.

Everybody knew Bill Walton. Basketball fans had been watching the big redhead since he burst on the scene as a sophomore at UCLA in 1971. He was all-everything for three years there, helping the UClans continue the basketball dynasty that had started in the early 1960's. Before Walton, UCLA had another supercenter, Lew Alcindor, who later changed his name, but not his game. As a pro, Alcindor, now known as Kareem Abdul-Jabbar, became an all-star performer right from his rookie year. People expected the same from Walton.

But it didn't happen that way. It took Bill Walton three years to establish himself as an NBA superstar. It wasn't lack of talent. Bill always had that. Rather it was a combination of things, beginning with a series of injuries that didn't allow Bill to get fully in shape or to get really into the flow of NBA basketball.

There were other problems. The Blazers were an expansion franchise. When Bill joined them in 1974, it was just the fifth year of their existence. The franchise was still building, going through the musical chairs of player changes that always characterize new teams.

There were other complications. While Bill Walton was at UCLA, fans outside California simply regarded him as a great basketball player. But those closest to him and the team knew that on the other side of the rebounds, blocked shots, clutch baskets, and floor leadership was a very complex young man, a young man with strong ideas and opinions on many subjects, a young man who wanted to live his life a certain way.

When Bill was drafted by Portland, his celebrity status quickly reached larger proportions as hordes of ambitious reporters sought out the youngster and tried to dig deep into his inner motivations. For instance, as soon as Bill finished his senior year at UCLA, he let his flaming red hair grow long and wild, something UClan coach John Wooden had not permitted. He began to grow a beard (something not uncommon among NBA centers). Though he had been a vegetarian for several years, his diet suddenly became an issue: some people said he wouldn't have the weight or strength to survive the rigors of NBA play. The controversy was starting.

Bill didn't enjoy talking to reporters even then, especially when they asked personal questions unrelated to basketball. But when his opinions did begin to appear in newspapers and magazines, the average sports fan began to wonder what this 6-11 redhead was all about.

For instance, after observing professional sports for a time, Walton remarked, "There are a lot of things wrong with professional athletics. But changes are going to come slowly since the people who are associated with the big business elements of sports are calling the shots now. But I'm not going to let the sports establishment impose their ideas on me.

"I feel," he went on, "that the place of sports in society should be as a means of drawing people from different backgrounds closer together, a means of having fun, and a means of promoting better health . . . for the masses, not just for a few."

Although he acknowledged that he played basketball to win, Bill also felt the game meant more than winning or losing. In other words, he played the game for the game's sake. "If you play good, you feel good," he said. "If you play badly, you don't feel so good. But there's always tomorrow and another game. It's fun to win, but I don't let it make me incredibly high. And I don't let losing bring me way down. I get high on playing the game and playing it right."

When the injuries began to mount his rookie year, Bill made good his threat not to let the establishment impose their ways on him. Much to the chagrin of Blazer fans and some of his teammates, he refused to go along with standard medical practices. "Doctors tend to experiment on athletes," he said bluntly. "There has been little research done on the effects of pain-killing drugs like cortisone and butazolodin. I'm not about to risk my body on someone's experiments. I'll make my own decisions as I go along."

It's not difficult to see how the great Walton controversy got started. And there's much more. But first it's necessary to go back to the beginning and see just how Bill Walton got to be where he is today.

Born on November 5, 1952, in La Mesa, California, William Theodore Walton III was one of four children born to Ted and Gloria Walton. His brother Bruce, older by just a year, is a 6-6, 250-pound mammoth of a man who was a star tackle at UCLA and spent several years in the NFL. Cathy Walton, a year younger than Bill, played center on a women's basketball team, while the youngest boy, Andy, is 6-5 and also a ballplayer.

Yet there was no push into athletics in the Walton household. Though Ted Walton was a husky 6-4, he preferred to steer his children into music. Everyone in the family sang or played an instrument, and the clan often gathered around the piano evenings and enjoyed each other's company in a round of playing and singing. "I didn't push my kids into sports," says Mr. Walton. "I only encouraged them to play as a broadening experience to complement their music. Wouldn't you know it that all of them gave up music and wound up in sports."

There was also a longtime social awareness in the Walton family. Mr. Walton was a district chief for the San Diego Department of Public Welfare, and Mrs. Walton was a librarian. Both were always conscious of the needs of the poor and underprivileged. As one of his friends once said, "Ted gets involved personally with a good many of our cases. He is especially interested in the Aid to Dependent Children program and does everything he can to see that these kids are provided for, that they can get an education."

Obviously there was a lot of serious talk in the Walton home, since parents and children were a close-knit family group who spent a great deal of time together. Coming from this kind of background and growing up in the socially conscious California atmosphere of the late 1960's and early 1970's, it is not really surprising that Bill turned out as he did.

Of course, Bill's social growth and development were accompanied by his physical growth. All the Waltons had huge appetites; when Mrs. Walton put the family spread down each day, it must have looked as if she were preparing to feed an army. These were Bill's pre-vegetarian days, and the kids sometimes dined on hamburgers and hot dogs for breakfast, while dinner almost always consisted of a huge roast or several steaks plus all the trimmings. Even today, vegetarian Bill remembers those times. "There's no doubt in my mind that Glo's cooking is one of the reasons I grew to be 6-11," he has said.

Bill attended Blessed Sacrament School in San Diego and as a grade schooler began playing all the sports, as had older brother Bruce before him. His first coach was a man named Frank Graziano, a fireman who loved teaching kids sports and received only gasoline money for his efforts. But watching youngsters like Bill grow to love sports and become better at them was payment enough.

By the time Bill reached eighth grade he was an outstanding football player as well as a basketball star. But Frank Graziano had more foresight than many a part-time grade school coach. Though long-and-lanky Bill was a fine end on the football team, Graziano convinced the youngster to forget high school football and concentrate on the court game. Though just barely six feet tall in eighth grade, Bill played center on defense for Blessed Sacrament. Because he was also the team's best ball handler, Graziano had him play guard on offense. He already played the all-around game. No wonder his coach wanted him to concentrate on basketball.

Bill moved on to Helix High School, where he concentrated on basketball, as Coach Graziano had advised. He didn't mind, because by this time he loved the game more than anything else. He was, however, getting to the age where he was beginning to grow, but yet wasn't too strong. He was already playing on a gimpy left knee that was so bad he had to undergo surgery at the end of his freshman year for the repair of a torn cartilage. An operation at such a tender age can discourage some boys from further competition. But not Bill.

When he came back as a sophomore, he had to take it easy as the knee slowly regained its strength. Because of this, he wasn't in top shape and spent a good deal of the season on the junior varsity team. He did play six varsity games near the end of the year, prompting Coach Gordon Nash to say: "For a sophomore with no experience he rebounded pretty well."

That wasn't much, but it was a start. Something else was happening too. Bill began his sophomore season at 6-1. But when he came back to the team as a junior he stood 6-7. Such rapid growth is not uncommon among very tall boys, happening to most of basketball's big men at about this same age. At any rate, Coach Nash now had a luxury, the tall and slender Bill Walton and the 6-5, 283-pound Bruce Walton both on the same team. He had a high-low post offense featuring the Walton brothers, who certainly looked like basketball's strangest brother act. The taller Bill weighed about 100 pounds less than his football-playing brother.

The difference went deeper than appearance. Bill's lack of weight made it difficult for him to go the whole game. "He'd often get tired," said his coach, "but he'd always tell me, and I'd take him out for a breather." When he was in there, Bill was an effective scorer and rebounder. Sometimes the opposition tried to stop him with strong-arm tactics, but Bill had a solution for that, too. His brother Bruce remembers, "When they'd begin to rough Bill up," says Bruce, "he'd look at me and I'd look at the coach. When the coach gave me the nod I'd wait until the ref wasn't looking and then let the guy know in my own way that he'd better not mess with my kid brother."

The team had a 29-2 record that year and won the CIF championship of the San Diego section, beating more than 50 schools for that honor.

The next year, 1969-70, Bruce had graduated to UCLA and its football program. But Bill didn't really need his protection anymore. He had grown to 6-10½ and was filling out. He worked on his stamina by taking long bicycle rides around San Diego. He was much more confident. "I was older and smarter," he recalls. "Plus I had put on about 15 pounds and had learned not to waste so much energy on the floor."

Once the season started, Bill went on a rampage and didn't stop. He was everywhere, directing the Helix team on both offense and defense. He was the hub on both ends of the floor. And he didn't just dunk the ball. He hit on a variety of jumpers and hooks as well as dunk shots. He had also developed the uncanny instinct and split-second timing that has made him a top rebounder.

Neither he nor the Helix team stopped until they had won 33 straight games and had captured another CIF title. As for Bill, he had averaged 29 points and 22.4 rebounds a game. He also made 70 percent of his shots and left high school having been on the winning side in his final 49 ball games.

The question was now which college he would choose. Anyone who saw him realized his great skills and tremendous potential. In fact, a former NBA player and coach, Jack McMahon, saw him play at Helix his senior year and said he was ready for the pros right then and there. "I was never so impressed by a player who was so accomplished so young," McMahon said.

But strangely enough, Bill was not the most celebrated big man to be entering college that year. Many so-called experts thought a 6-10 youngster named Tom

McMillen was destined to become college basketball's next supercenter. McMillen did go on to a fine career at Maryland, but his accomplishments fell far short of Bill's.

At any rate, midway through Bill's senior year, the phone calls and letters from the colleges started coming. Coach Nash, as well as the Walton family, was inundated by them. Soon the recruiters were coming in person, many of them wanting to wine and dine the entire Walton family. But Ted Walton gave them the same answer—a polite "no thanks!" "Ted has a lot of character," said one of his friends. "He didn't want to feel obligated to the recruiters in any way. He felt it was better like that."

Those recruiters the Waltons wanted to know better, however, were invited to the Walton home for dinner. "It's a tradition we began when Bruce was being recruited for football," said Mr. Walton. "And it was something we enjoyed doing, plus it gave the boys a chance to really talk to whoever we had over." The guests during Bill's senior year included Johnny Dee of Notre Dame, Bob Boyd of USC, and John Wooden of UCLA. Perhaps UCLA had the advantage right from the start. For one thing, brother Bruce had gone there to play football. Second, there was the great basketball tradition, and Coach Wooden was a big part of it.

Wooden's first national title came in 1963-64 with a quick, well-disciplined team led by a pair of all-American guards, Walt

Hazzard and Gail Goodrich, and a fine forward, Keith Erickson. The team won it without an outstanding center, then repeated the next season with the same type of club. They didn't win it in 1965-66. But the next year along came the 7-2 Lew Alcindor, and the UClans won three straight championships with Alcindor dominating everyone. In the next two seasons, 1969-70 and 1970-71, the club had an average center, Steve Patterson, but two great forwards, Sidney Wicks and Curtis Rowe, plus the usual quick guards. The result was two more national titles, which made five in a row and seven in eight years. Now Walton was coming, and everyone figured the dynasty would continue.

Bill, of course, didn't make a hasty decision. He thought it all over very carefully before announcing his decision to go to Westwood and UCLA. "I felt they offered the best combination of academics and athletics," said Bill. He wasn't kidding. His studies were very important to him; he wasn't just going to college to play ball and get ready for the pros. He also knew that two other fine high school players, Greg Lee and Keith Wilkes, were headed for UCLA, and he liked that idea. Even then Bill was a team player and wanted a good supporting cast around him.

As a freshman Bill lived up to all expectations. He led the Bruin frosh to a perfect 20-0 record, averaging 18 points and grabbing 16 rebounds per game. With Wicks,

Rowe, and Patterson graduating, there'd be virtually a new varsity team in 1971-72. But with Walton coming up, the excitement at Westwood was building all over again.

Bill and his teammates didn't disappoint. They began winning with relative ease. Walton and Wilkes made immediate contributions, but there were others. Senior guard Henry Bibby, the only starter back from the year before, provided leadership. Other outstanding players were Tommy Curtis, Larry Hollyfield, and Larry Farmer. The Bruins were so deep that Bill's backup center was a seven-footer named Swen Nater. Nater rarely played in his three years at Westwood, but was highly regarded and has gone on to become a very good pro center in the NBA.

At any rate, the unbeaten Bruins jumped to the top of the basketball rankings and people began reading about the team's new supercenter, Bill Walton. Some people were already comparing him to such dominating centers as Bill Russell and Wilt Chamberlain, as well as to his predecessor at UCLA, Kareem Abdul-Jabbar.

Despite his height, Bill was an extremely mobile center. He was all over the court—blocking shots, tipping in shots, grabbing rebounds, chasing loose balls, and playing the key role in the UCLA 2-2-1 zone press. His teammate and friend, Greg Lee, talked about Bill's skills midway through his first varsity season. "You have to be a real student of the game to appreciate all the things Bill does," said Lee. "We're only now beginning to realize how good he is. With Bill back there on defense, we can afford to gamble and cheat, and we don't have to hesitate about getting out on our fast break." Similar things were said by members of the Boston Celtics when Bill Russell took over as their center.

Bruin Coach Wooden also began talking about his newest superstar. "Bill does so many things that don't show up in the box score," said the veteran coach. "Things like intimidation. How do you measure that? When we had Lewis [Alcindor], the other teams had a lower shooting percentage. It went back up for a couple of years after he graduated, but now with Bill, it will go down again. Our opponents this year are hitting in the high 30's and Bill is greatly responsible for that. Not only because of the shots he blocks, but because they are always looking for him, just as they used to look for Lewis all the time."

As always, it was team basketball that turned Bill on the most. He explained part of it to one reporter. "On defense I make a point of knowing where all my guys are, all the time," he said. "So that way, when I get the ball, even if I'm facing the basket, I can be thinking about the fast break. I know Henry is over here and Keith is close by and Larry [Farmer] is at least within 10 feet of me. When I get the ball out, then trail the play and see everything materialize in front of me—Wow! That pleases me more than anything." Coach Wooden confirmed this quality in Bill. "Bill loves the game, but only as a team game. He's very impatient and gets upset when he feels the game isn't being played right. That's what bothers him the most."

Bill didn't have too many upsets as a sophomore. The Bruins continued to steamroll their opponents, and the club was already being compared favorably to the UCLA title teams of the past. But, as the season wore on, people began to learn more about the real Bill Walton. And they were fast finding out that he wasn't your ordinary, run-of-the-mill basketball star.

"I realize that I can't keep my whole life private," he said during his sophomore year. "My basketball life is open to everyone, but what I do off the court for my own recreation and entertainment is my own business. I do what I want to do and people don't have to know about it. Even Coach Wooden doesn't always know what I do.

"Everybody expects me to be a certain way. They have their own ideas of what a college ballplayer should be like, with the short hair and all that. They think the UCLA team is a bunch of all-American-boy types, but we're not. I'm trying to have fun in life and not worry what other people think."

Bill didn't like big parties or gatherings. He preferred to spend his time in a quiet place, perhaps talking with a small handful of friends. He had a steady girl who continued to be a constant companion right on into his professional days. He carefully protected her from the press and other people who might try to bother or exploit her.

There were other things occupying Bill's mind. He had observed that the varsity the year before was broken up into small groups, much of it along black-white lines. Even though the team had won the national title, they were not a close group. Bill didn't want it that way when he joined the varsity. He knew the key would be Bibby, the only starter from the previous team and a black man. "The guys on our freshman team were all very close," Bill said. "I knew them very well. The only possible problem I thought we might have would be with Henry. He'd be the top man, the senior, and he could have easily played the Mr. Cool or Mr. Above Everything role. But he didn't. He's our leader and I have the greatest respect for him. If Henry told me I was shooting too much or something like that, I'd stop.

"But it's really a lot of fun playing with the guys we have. If I had played on last year's team I know I wouldn't have liked it. But I want to play with these guys as long as I can. I don't want to play with some guys who are 40." The last remarks were meant to quell any rumors that Bill might leave UCLA early to turn pro. He felt he was committed to the UClans for three years, and he also wanted to finish his education.

Bill also had strong views on the race question in America. He took courses in Afro-American studies and was fully sympathetic to the black man's plight in America. As one reporter said, "Bill's black teammates have always considered him a blue-eyed brother." Bill himself once said, "I don't blame the blacks for hating whites. They've gotten such a raw deal for so long." He also once added that he sympathized with blacks' aspirations, understood their frustrations, and wouldn't blame a black man for killing him! That's strong stuff, the kind that most people don't like to hear about their sports idols. But Bill never took a backward step from his convictions. And at UCLA his basketball always got the number one headlines.

The team continued to march through its opponents. But as the season wore on, Bill began to suffer physically. He was so good that many opponents took to pounding him under the boards whenever they could. In an 81-56 win over USC, Bill took a tremendous beating. Both his knees were sore—tendonitis the doctors said. Yet he held each of the USC centers to two points each. In January the club had to play Stanford on a Friday night and Cal on Saturday afternoon. It wasn't easy.

"That weekend really messed up my legs," said Bill. "I need more than 15 hours between games to be ready to play again. The pain didn't go away for quite a while. Then I got something wrong with my big toes. The tendons were torn in them from jumping. As a center, I don't do that much running, but a lot of quick jumping. I had to have cortisone shots for my toes and started taking medicine to reduce inflammation." Those were the days before Bill refused that kind of medication.

Bill pulled himself together, however, and led the Bruins to an unbeaten season. In a February game against Oregon he had a high of 37 points. And in the NCAA playoffs he was equally brilliant, leading the Bruins to another national title. In 30 games, Bill had 633 points for a 21.1 average and grabbed 466 rebounds for an average of 15.5 a game. He was everybody's all-America and college basketball's Player of the Year.

The next year it was more of the same. The Bruins were a smooth-working machine that steamrolled their opponents. Once again they rolled to the national championship, their seventh in succession and ninth in 10 years. And once again Bill Walton was the best player in college basketball. If anyone had doubted it, they simply had to watch the NCAA final game, in which the Bruins faced a very strong Memphis State team. In that game Bill was absolutely devastating, his defense eliminating the Memphis State attack. And, for a change, he completely took charge on offense. He took 22 shots during the game, made 21 of them (Yes, 21 of them!), and added a pair of free throws. The big guy ended up with 44 points—a new championship scoring record for UCLA—as the Bruins won easily.

Counting his freshman year and a pair of 30-win seasons following, Bill had helped win 80 straight games since arriving at Westwood. When the 49 straight his Helix High team had accumulated were added on, Bill Walton had been on the winning side in 129 straight basketball games—an amazing feat.

More of the same was expected when Bill returned to UCLA for his final year, once again putting aside any rumors that he would turn pro. But some also said that the team wasn't as strong as it had been the previous two years. Walton and Wilkes were back, and the club had another fine forward in Dave Meyers. But what seemed to be lacking was firepower from the guard position. If the front line could be shut down somehow, perhaps the Bruins could be stopped.

But the Bruins once again were winning; despite a few close calls they were again number one. When they arrived in South Bend late in January to play Notre Dame, the Bruins had won 88 straight games. In fact, the last team that had beaten them was Notre Dame, back on January 23, 1971. This time the Irish were ready once again. They were also unbeaten and contesting the Bruins for the number one ranking.

The one problem with the Bruins was Bill. He had sustained a back injury some 12 days earlier and had missed a couple of games. Now he was back, but some people wondered how he'd be fixed for stamina if the game had a furious pace and was close at the end.

For the first 14 minutes of the game the Bruins looked unbeatable. Walton was getting the boards, and the UCLA fast break was working. In addition, the Bruin defense kept the Irish from penetrating, and the Notre Dame shooters couldn't hit from the outside. With six minutes left in the first half, UCLA had a 17-point lead, and it seemed as if the rout was on.

But the Irish hung in there. They kept the score respectable well into the second half. Bill was playing well, though he did seem to be tiring a bit. Part of his fatigue probably was caused by the tenacious way Notre Dame's burly 6-9 center, John Shumate, was playing him. Shumate and the Notre Dame defense were keeping the ball away from Bill a good deal of the time.

Still, with three minutes left, the Bruins held a comfortable 70-59 lead. Then something happened that had never occurred before in Bill's years at UCLA. The Bruins lost their poise. They couldn't put the ball in the hoop and they were turning it over. Four times they gave it to the Irish without getting off a shot. Notre Dame was chipping away. Suddenly it was 70-65, then 70-67, and then 70-69. Notre Dame had the ball with just seconds left.

Notre Dame brought the ball up. They gave it to junior Dwight Clay near the right base line. He went up with a jump shot. SWISH! The Irish led, 71-70, and the place was in an uproar. UCLA had one last chance, but again they couldn't do anything. The clock ran out, and the winning streak was ended.

Bill had played well, considering his injury. He had 24 points on 12 of 14 from the floor. But Shumate also had 24, and the rest of the Irish simply outplayed the Bruins. The streak was over. Now the question was, could the Bruins bounce back?

A week later they had their chance. They met the Irish again, this time at their home arena, Pauley Pavilion. The Bruins were primed and ready and so was Bill. He wanted the ball and he got it, this time going over Shumate time and again. UCLA jumped off to a 9-0 lead, increased it to 43-30 at half time, and went on from there to take an easy 94-75 victory that once again put them atop the college ratings. Bill was totally dominant in the game, making 16 of 19 shots from the floor to finish with 32 points. After the game, Coach Wooden put it all into perspective with a few well-chosen words. "I think there are times when a loss can really help a team," he said.

There was another college team that year hoping the same philosophy would prove to be true for them—the North Carolina State Wolfpack, coached by Norm Sloan. A year earlier N.C. State challenged UCLA for the top spot among college fives. Like the Bruins, the Wolfpack were unbeaten in the regular season, finishing number two to UCLA in the polls. But because of some problems with the NCAA, N.C. State was banned from postseason tournament play and couldn't challenge the Bruins for the national crown.

But they had a powerful team led by a brilliant, high-leaping forward, David Thompson, and a 7-4 giant center, Tom Burleson. This year State hoped things would be different when they met UCLA early in the regular season.

The game turned into a travesty. The Walton Gang, as some liked to call the Bruins, blew the Wolfpack out, 84-66. There didn't seem to be any doubt about which was the better team. But then State rebounded and won the rest of its games. As the NCAA playoffs approached, both clubs had lost only a single game and were again ranked one and two in the country. It looked as if another showdown were approaching.

Sure enough, both clubs whipped through their tournament opponents and into the NCAA semifinals, where they would finally clash. The game took place on March 23, 1974, in Greensboro, North Carolina. If the Wolfpack had any advantage, it would be the crowd rooting heavily for the Carolina team.

Both clubs were sky-high for the game, battling evenly in the early going. Then, slowly, UCLA began to take a lead—not a big lead, but one that seemed to hold between five and 10 points. But the UClans couldn't seem to break it open. For one thing, the 7-4 Burleson, a good but not great center, was playing one of the best games of his life and battling Walton on fairly even terms.

Early in the second half UCLA spurted again, building their lead to 49-38. A couple more baskets, and they could put it away. Then N.C. State missed a shot, and Walton grabbed the rebound. But as he held the ball over his head, Burleson somehow plucked it out of his hands and put it in the hoop. Once again State had new life and battled back.

Then, with just 11 minutes left, the Bruins again built to an 11-point lead at 57-46; once again the experts felt the time had come. Only this time State's smallest man, 5-7 Monty Towe, ignited the Wolfpack fast break and State scored 10 straight points to make it 57-56. The teams then traded a couple of baskets, keeping the Bruins ahead, 61-60. At that point Thompson took charge, leaping to the rafters to put in a lob pass, getting fouled, and hitting the free throw. State had its first lead at 63-61. The Bruins were in a ball game and they knew it.

Each club was being careful now, holding the ball for the best possible shot. The score was tied at 65 with 51 seconds left. The ball went into Bill and he hooked. It bounced off the rim and Burleson grabbed the rebound. State played for the last shot and also missed. The game went into overtime.

The first OT period was a tentative, ball-holding one. Each club scored just one basket. State had another chance to win when they got the ball on a steal with 10 seconds left. Thompson passed to Burleson, who missed a short spin shot at the buzzer. It was still tied and going into a second overtime.

In the second OT the Bruins started running, and they quickly ran up a 74-67 lead. It looked as if they were ready to take charge, but the Wolfpack went into a press and began forcing errors. Once more they came back and closed the gap.

With 1:16 left UCLA led by one, 75-74, and Meyers was on the line with a one-on-one situation. He missed the first and State had the ball. Once again it was Thompson, taking charge and leaping high over Wilkes to hit a jumper, who put State ahead, 76-75. This time the UClans couldn't come back. Greg Lee missed a one-hander and Wilkes was called for a pushing foul. Thompson made both shots, upping the lead to 78-75. Seconds later Monty Towe hit two more free throws, and State led by five. Walton's 29th point of the night made it 80-77, but that's the way it ended. North Carolina State had ended UCLA's championship reign. Two nights later they became national champs by beating Marquette.

For UCLA and Bill Walton, it was the

end of an era. It was the kind of game Bill loved to play in, and he wasn't crushed by the loss. He knew what he had done in his three years and could hold his head high. In fact, when he left the arena that night, one of the workers approached him and asked to shake his hand. A lesser player or person might have brushed the man aside, but Bill just offered his hand and accepted the congratulations with a friendly "Thanks," adding, "And thanks for all you've done for us."

But it was college basketball that should have thanked Bill Walton. And they did by naming him Player of the Year once more. He also won the Sullivan Award as the outstanding amateur athlete of 1973. Those who had seen him play couldn't say enough about him. Many expected him to make whatever pro team he joined an instant winner, as Kareem Abdul-Jabbar had done with the Milwaukee Bucks several years earlier.

Bill knew he'd get offers from both the NBA and the rival ABA, and he kept quiet until the draft was completed. But there was never any question in his mind as to which league he'd choose. Despite getting a bigger offer from the ABA, Bill quickly said he'd play in Portland after that NBA team picked him. He said that he wanted to play against the best, and the only way he could really test himself was to accept the challenge of the NBA. He soon signed a long-term contract with the Trail Blazers for an estimated 2.5 million dollars.

Now the NBA just had to wait for Bill Walton. When he emerged for the exhibition season with Portland, he had changed markedly. He wasn't kidding about long hair. Once away from the UCLA rules, Bill had let his hair grow out and played with a headband to keep it in place. Later he'd even tie it in a ponytail. He also had a red beard growing down the sides of his face and around his chin. But that didn't bother people too much at first. What bothered Portland officials was Bill's weight. He had always played around 230 in college, but now he was down about 15 pounds. Right away they attributed it to his vegetarian diet, but Walton refused any suggestions that he begin eating "dead flesh" once again. "I used to eat hot dogs and ketchup and french fries and steak and junk like that," he said, bluntly. "I did that, and I know what that's like. Now I've done this, and I know this is definitely better.

"Most people in this country are junk food addicts," he continued, "and most junk foods are loaded with sugar, which has a damaging effect on the body. Most of the meat that is eaten contains poisons that are present because the animals have been shot up with steroids and other crap, force fed, and then brutally killed. A lot of other foods contain poisons as a result of having been processed and refined, which means that nutrition is taken out and restricting chemicals are put in." Most people didn't want to hear about

Bill's diet. But they'd put up with it as long as he produced on the court. That was the important thing.

Portland was badly in need of a winner. The team began in the 1970-71 season. They had the co-rookie of the Year that season in guard Geoff Petrie, who averaged 24.8 points a game. But the club was a big loser at 29-53. The next year Portland again drafted the Rookie of the Year, 6-9 Sidney Wicks from UCLA. When Petrie missed a good many games with a knee injury, Wicks took over with a 24.5 average. However, the team mark got even worse at 18-64.

The next year the two stars were on the court at the same time, but rarely played team ball. It seemed to be a contest as to who would get the most shots. Both averaged more than 20 a game, but the Trail Blazers managed just a 21-61 record. The fans of Portland were getting restless.

In 1973-74, the Blazers managed just a 27-55 mark. It was the fourth year of their existence, and they still hadn't matched the losing record of their first year. Fewer and fewer fans were coming out to see the team play . . . until it was announced that the club had drafted and signed Bill Walton. Suddenly sales were up and more and more people bought season tickets. If Walton could just fit in with Wicks and Petrie, the Blazers might become a winner.

But the NBA has a history of teams with three so-called superstars not working well together. The last example was the Los Angeles Lakers, when they acquired Wilt Chamberlain to go with Jerry West and Elgin Baylor. The team became a champion only when Baylor was forced into retirement by an injury. Teamwork and unselfishness were still the proven trademarks in the league, as perhaps best exemplified by the long dynasty of the Boston Celtics.

At any rate, those who knew him realized that Bill was a team ballplayer. And if Petrie and Wicks were just looking for their own shots, the whole thing could turn Walton off.

Bill's pro debut came in an exhibition game against the L.A. Lakers. Though slender-looking and somewhat gaunt, Bill was simply devastating. He controlled the game at both ends of the court, much as he had done at UCLA. His teammates and Coach Lenny Wilkins were simply delighted. Bill was all over the court. He was quick and agile and seemed to go all out on every play. When it ended the Blazers had a 92-91 victory, with Bill scoring 26 points and gathering in an incredible 28 rebounds.

But if Bill had been inclined to gloat over his initial success, he was in store for a rude awakening. Shortly after that Lakers meeting, Portland rolled into Dayton, Ohio, for an exhibition game against the Milwaukee Bucks and Kareem Abdul-Jabbar. The press played the game up, making it a contest between the king and the heir apparent. But what it quickly turned into was a basketball lesson given by Mr. Abdul-Jabbar to young Mr. Walton.

Two minutes into the game Kareem went to work. First it was a short jumper, then a stuff, another jumper, a lay-up, a hook. He was doing it all with ease, a bored expression on his face, while Walton moved from place to place in vain, trying to find a way to stop the big man. Then with one second left in the quarter, Kareem picked up the ball some 15 feet from the hoop and casually hit a beautiful sky hook at the buzzer.

Bill just stood and stared as the Buck's center walked off. That's the way it continued when the two men were on the court together. During the 27 minutes that they went head to head, Kareem outscored Bill, 28-8. Some observers were quick to point out that Walton had outrebounded Kareem, 16-11, suggesting that the youngster was a more aggressive and natural rebounder (something that has proven true in subsequent seasons). The ease with which Abdul-Jabbar scored, however, might have had a serious effect on Bill, who, when it was over, simply said: "I've said it before and I'll say it again, he's the best I've ever seen. I really learned something out there tonight."

Soon after that game Bill's performance began to suffer. Other centers were scoring on him and, more important, physically pushing him around. Once again people criticized his diet and claimed he was too frail for NBA play. But one of Bill's friends thought it was more than that. "Bill was really depressed after the game against Kareem," the man said. "He felt as if he was really whipped and this was something he wasn't used to. After that, players started pushing him around like a sheet of paper and he hardly fought back. It seemed as if his desire was fading fast."

Perhaps Bill had failed to heed a warning given him by John Wooden before he left UCLA. The wily coach had told his star that "the emotional and not the physical part of the pro game would be difficult, that in the pros it's not basically a team game." Wooden continued. "I also felt Bill would need discipline, a firm hand underneath it all. We had our disagreements when he was here, but I always governed his behavior and appearance on the court. There's no one to tell him 'no' on the Trail Blazers."

The long-drawn-out speculation as to what was wrong with Bill Walton was beginning. Some said he was used to being the leader, and, as the youngest player on the Blazers, he was often the butt of jokes. With his beard, hair, and mountain-man-type clothes, his teammates had plenty of ammunition.

Bill also began to resent the press, whose members often referred to him as "The Great White Hope," the first really good white center to come along in some time. Bill often railed against this, saying, "If I were black, I'd be just another center."

It also became apparent early in the season that the Blazers hadn't lost their tendency to regard team play as a plague. Petrie and Wicks were still firing away at will, and that, too, was getting to Bill. In one game, Petrie took a very long shot. Bill grabbed the rebound, but instead of going back up with it he immediately called a timeout. Word was that in the huddle he announced he couldn't play that kind of selfish basketball anymore.

As the regular season started Bill and the Blazers were not playing well. The team was expected to win and it wasn't. In addition, Bill seemed to tire late in the game, prompting more talk about his diet and apparently continuing weight loss. Coach Wilkens explained it away, however, by saying, "A lot of rookies run out of stamina."

Then he started to miss games. First it was a pair when he got the flu. After that he jammed the little finger of his left hand and stayed out a week. The critics jumped on him, saying it wasn't his shooting hand, and that pros have played with broken, let alone jammed, fingers. When he finally returned it took just two more games for him to begin to complain about a bone spur on his foot. The spur kept him out of more and more games. When asked about it, Bill would simply say, "It hurts." Yet many people, including some of Bill's teammates, were quick to point out that bone spurs were a common ailment for basketball players, and many players managed to play with them, to play with the pain.

Dr. Robert Kerlan, a top sports doctor and surgeon, had treated Bill at UCLA. Kerlan pointed out again that most players have spurs, that they result from running and cutting, and that they usually occur on the ankle that the players pivots on the most. But Kerlan also added, "Bill certainly showed in college that he could play with pain. I know that for a fact. Perhaps he just does not prefer to play with this particular injury."

Yet the speculation grew that Walton's injury wasn't as bad as he led people to believe. Some teammates said they saw him jogging freely, and before one game he was playing one-on-one against another rookie, only to appear on the bench in street clothes when the game began. Once on the bench he didn't seem to care whether the Blazers won or lost. Later he explained his apparent indifference. "I love basketball," he said, "and I wish more than anything else that I could be playing right now. But I'm injured and I can't. When I am playing I get very emotionally involved both in practice and in games, and in talking about it. But when I'm not playing I don't. It's probably my way of controlling the frustrations of not playing."

But that didn't help matters with the fans, who were now booing Bill, or with his teammates, who wondered about his desire. As it turned out, the so-called bone spur was found to be strained ankle ligaments which required a walking cast—a legitimate injury.

That wasn't all. The more they knew him,

the more his mates and others found Bill to be a strange person. Some said he was at least a seven-footer, but that he insisted on being listed at 6-11 because he felt that seven feet was where being a freak started.

In addition he was constantly talking about California, how great everything was in his home state. The feeling was that Bill was angling for a trade to his hometown Lakers. There were rumors that he was looking for a way to break his contract and that he was even threatening to quit. Yet when Bill first came to Oregon he loved the area and began building a large A-frame house in the woods. He loved the sun, which he said gave him energy, and the smog-free climate. He was quoted as saying that he "may never go to Southern California again."

That was before the long Oregon winter set in. Unlike California, where the sun keeps shining, the old bright ball takes a holiday in Oregon. The winters are often rainy and damp. Bill began complaining about the lack of sun. He said on more than one occasion, "I just can't get warm here. My feet are always cold. When is it going to warm up?" And he dressed as if he were going to Alaska.

When he did return to the lineup, he wasn't in top shape and was a little more than a part-time player. There were those occasional flashes of brilliance, reminders of what could be; but it was obvious that both his physical and mental condition wouldn't allow him to be the player he was in college. He surely wasn't about to turn the franchise around, and he must have wondered himself if he'd ever play top-notch NBA basketball.

By the end of the season many people were regarding him as no more than a hippie, a long-haired Commie bum, and worse. The Blazers got a little better, finishing at 38-44, but as guard Geoff Petrie said, "The season was a disaster. Bill was a real disappointment in his attitude and how he behaved. There were times when he didn't act as if he wanted to play. He didn't like the team or the city. He was aloof. We didn't think he was faking his injuries, but we all wanted him to play so badly because we were thinking about winning a championship with him, and the thing blew up in our faces." When it was over, Bill had played in just 35 of the team's 82 games. His scoring average was 12.8 a game, and his rebounding average was nearly the same, 12.6. That was the only good sign: he could still get that ball. But everything else was disappointing.

Trail Blazer fans were hoping again when the 1975-76 season approached. What kind of condition would Bill be in? Bill tried to show he hadn't lost his enthusiasm for the game. At one point he explained how he felt to a reporter. "I've played all the sports," he said, "baseball, football, tennis, track, and it just seems that basketball is the most complete game because it requires the most skills. It's a game I'm built for, but even if I were short I think I could make it as a guard."

But Bill was also continuing his so-called counterculture life-style. He spoke out on political issues and, at one point, was indirectly involved in the sordid Patty Hearst affair when some of his friends were allegedly implicated. It got to the point where the FBI was supposedly nosing around Bill's house. But nothing ever came of that, except that Walton was as controversial as ever.

Then there was a new physical problem. During the off-season Bill broke a bone in his foot on a lawn sprinkler chasing a frisbee. Once again he came to camp in less than top condition. The year before he had been recovering from an early summer knee operation. And when a player is not in top shape, his play becomes tired, making the chance of injury much greater.

In a sense, much of Bill's second season resembled his first. He didn't miss as many games, but he continued to incur injuries and lose time, valuable experience, and conditioning. He was still thin and still prone to complain about Portland, the team, and various other things. Everybody took potshots at him to the point where one of the league's PR directors called him "the most maligned, castigated athlete since Muhammad Ali."

Through it all, the Blazers continued to hover below .500 as a team. Many of the same problems remained. Although Wicks and Petrie were still the team's top scorers, they couldn't seem to make basketball music together. And not knowing who the center would be from game to game didn't make things easier.

The coaching staff, as well as players around the league, had seen enough of Bill to know that the potential was still there. But Assistant Coach Tom Meschery, a former NBA forward, had one doubt. "I wasn't sure that Bill was mean enough for the NBA," said Meschery. The 6-6 Meschery wasn't a finesse player in his day; he did it on blood and guts. To keep in shape, he often worked out with the team, and he intentionally gave Bill quite a battering underneath. One day the two became involved in a one-on-one game. It was getting rougher, Meschery dishing out the elbows and hips. Finally Bill had enough. He drove straight at Meschery, and before the coach could move, had run right over him, leaving Meschery with a bloody nose.

Bill didn't even apologize, but Meschery didn't care. Despite the bloody nose, he had a big grin on his face. The question of Bill's meanness had been answered. Meschery had other good things to say about Bill—things he had seen when Bill was healthy. "Compared to most NBA players," said Meschery, "Bill lives like a Boy Scout, and the harder we work him in practice the more he loves it. I've never met anyone quite like him. We'd be in great shape if everybody on the team had his attitude, never mind his ability."

It was good to hear something positive said about Bill. Unfortunately, he couldn't stay healthy long enough to shut the other mouths. A broken wrist, major injury of the season, helped put him on the shelf for another 31 games. Yet, in the 51 games in which he did play that year, his game improved. His scoring average was up to 16.1 and he grabbed 681 rebounds for an average of 13.3 a game.

Many people made light of Bill's fracture because it was of the left wrist, not his shooting hand. Old-timers remembered guys like Dolph Schayes and Bob Petit playing with similar injuries, using the casts on their wrists like clubs. In fact, Bill did play some games toward the end of the year when he thought the wrist was healing. But the injury was too serious. An off-season operation was necessary to insert a screw in the bone to make it heal correctly. According to some close friends, if the operation hadn't been successful, his career could have been ended.

Though he had to wear a cast on his wrist most of the summer, Bill nevertheless ran. He ran and ran and ran. He played several hours of soccer each day. In addition, though still adhering to his vegetarian diet, Bill ate more food to add bulk. So when he came to camp for the 1976-77 season, he was not only in great physical shape: he had beefed up to 240 pounds. He knew it was a pivotal season for him.

There were other reasons that Bill was

looking forward to the upcoming season. Blazer officials decided to rebuild the team. When the club had its sixth straight losing season in 1975-76, finishing at 37-45, many people suggested the club trade Walton while he still had some value. But the powers that be in Portland decided just the opposite. They decided to build the club around *him*.

One of the first moves was to change the coaching staff. Jack Ramsay, who had been a highly successful college coach at St. Joseph's of Philadelphia before a so-so couple of years at Buffalo, took over as head coach. One casualty of that change was Tom Meschery, who had some parting words in the way of a prediction. "I'll tell you what hurts about this," said Tom. "Bill Walton has been put through hell for the past two years, but now he's ready to do things on the court that have never been done before in the history of the NBA. No one deserves the success he's going to have more than Bill, and not being around to watch it after the agony he's gone through the last two years is just tearing me apart."

But there had to be some other changes before Bill could really do his thing. Fortunately, the Blazers were willing to make them. On August 25, 1976, the club announced a trade with the Atlanta Hawks. All the Blazers received was the Hawks's number two choice in the dispersal draft of ABA players. In turn, they gave up Petrie and forward Steve Hawes. It didn't seem like much until the Blazers used that draft choice to pick Maurice Lucas, a 6-9 power forward who would play brilliantly alongside Bill.

On September 1, the team announced a second major deal that sent Sidney Wicks packing. In less than one week the Trail Blazers had given up the two players who had been the mainstays of the franchise since its formation. The two had, however, also caused many problems for the club.

The trades allowed some other changes to occur. With Petrie gone second-year-man Lionel Hollins now led the backcourt. He was joined by ABA refugee Dave Twardzik, rookie speedster Johnny Davis, and veteran guard Herm Gilliam. Wicks's departure not only made room for Lucas; it also would give second-year-man Bobby Gross more playing time. Lloyd Neal remained on the club to back up Bill at center and also play forward. Veteran Larry Steele and two rookies rounded out the new Blazer squad.

There were certainly fewer stars on the club when the season began. In fact, with Bill's history of injuries, he couldn't even be considered a star. So it was a team of unknown quantity. But one important thing had changed: for the first time the Blazers would act and play as a *team*.

Bill and his new teammates worked hard in the exhibitions to learn about each other. Bill was playing brilliantly, doing the things that had always been expected of him. He was scoring, but only as much as was necessary. It was his defense, his rebounding, shotblocking, and his floor leadership that were really impressive. He quickly formed a close alliance with Lucas, also a vegetarian. But more important than that, Lucas was as tough as nails, a strong rebounder and 20-point scorer. They were a devastating combination up front.

Another change in Bill saw him spending more time with his teammates. He genuinely liked the new players and didn't shun public restaurants anymore. He was still careful what he ordered, but he wanted to be close to the players. It was more like UCLA now, and Bill was once again a leader. "This is the way it was in college," he said. "These are the kind of guys I'm used to playing with. This is going to be fun!"

Walton observers noticed a change on the court. They said that Bill was again curling his upper lip over his teeth and getting that glazed look in his eye. When he did that at UCLA, they always knew he was ready to play.

The Blazers started fast. They won four of their first five games. It was a new-look team all right. With Walton playing spectacularly, triggering the fast break and passing like a guard, the Blazers looked as good as any club in the league. But on November 5, they had a big test. They faced Julius Erving, George McGinnis, and the rest of the

Philadelphia 76ers. What's more, the game was played on Bill's 24th birthday.

The Coliseum in Portland was sold out for the contest days before the game. Philadelphia brought the crowd to its feet in the warm-ups, putting on a slam-dunk show featuring the Doctor, McGinnis, and centers Caldwell Jones and Darryl Dawkins. But once the game started, it was the Blazers who did the entertaining.

Hollins started it with a jumper over Doug Collins. Then big Lucas went to work, hitting seven straight points and giving Portland a solid lead. Minutes later Erving got the ball, drove past Gross to the hoop. That is when the Doctor is at his best. As Erving leaped in the air, Bill went up with him. The Doctor then went into his act: he switched hands, pumped once, and then went in, hanging in the air through it all. But somehow Bill stayed up with him. And when Erving finally shot, Bill was there to smash the ball back to the court. The Portland crowd went berserk.

From there the Blazers got better and better. They just blew Philly out, winning by a 146-104 score. Bill played just 32 minutes, yet hit 10 of 13 from the floor and six of seven from the line for 26 points. He also had 16 rebounds and six assists. What a birthday present he had given himself! After the game, George McGinnis spoke admiringly of Bill. "He did everything," said big George. "But he did it within a team concept. That's what impressed me the most. He's a total team player."

From there the Blazers rolled. They took over first place in their division and continued to play team ball. They had a balanced attack, led by Lucas and Walton. Bill was also leading the entire NBA in rebounding and blocked shots, while Lucas was among the top rebounders. Hollins was becoming a formidable guard, and Bobby Gross was doing an outstanding job at the small forward. What's more, the Portland bench was producing, Coach Ramsay making sure that everyone got playing time. That always makes for a happy family.

Bill was also happy with his new coach. In fact, Knicks General Manager Eddie Donovan credited Ramsay with Bill's new attitude and inspired play. "I think Ramsay reached Walton," said Donovan. "Of all the coaches in our league, Jack Ramsay is the closest to being the John Wooden type—scholarly, available. I think Walton responded to that."

As midseason approached the Blazers continued to lead their division. Bill was chosen the starting center on the West All-Star team, and many people were beginning to compare him with the other great centers of the game—Bill Russell, Wilt Chamberlain, and Kareem Abdul-Jabbar.

In the second half Bill continued to play outstanding basketball. But then it happened: a sprained left ankle. This time no one accused Bill of dogging it; he was on the bench and dying to get back in there. With no Walton the Blazers began to struggle, and once again became a less than .500 team. And while Bill was on the shelf, the L.A. Lakers took over the division lead. They did it primarily because of Kareem, who was having another great season and single-handedly making L.A. a winner.

Bill missed 17 games. During that time the Blazers had just a 5-12 record. It proved his value all over again. With Bill in the lineup, Portland had one of the best teams in the NBA; without him they were an also-ran. Philadelphia's George McGinnis summed up the change in Bill. "First of all, he's healthy," said McGinnis. "You can't play good if you don't feel good. But it's more than that. Last year he wouldn't get the ball. Now when he asks for it he gets it. There's no doubt in anybody's mind who the man is. When you're the man, you put out special. I heard one guy on television say he saw Walton's talent all the time. Who in the hell didn't see it?"

Bill came back to the lineup before the season ended and helped the Blazers put a lock on second place. His ankle was still tender, but he was determined to play with it. He felt he owed it to himself, his teammates, and the fans. And speaking of the fans, Bill really appreciated them. "They seem to get satisfaction out of more than just us winning games," he said. "They like good basketball, good basketball by both teams. And they don't have antagonism for our opponents. That's always nice to see."

When it ended, Portland had a 49-33 record, four games behind the Lakers in the Pacific Division. Had Bill not been injured, the Blazers would have probably finished on top. But by any previous standards, the season was an overwhelming success.

As for Bill, he really did the job. In 65 games he scored 1,210 points for an 18.6 average, second on the club to Lucas' 20.2 mark. In addition, he had the best rebounding average in the league, grabbing 934 for a 14.4 average. He also was tops in blocked shots with 211 and a 3.2 mark per game. Moreover, he was named the center of the NBA All-Defensive team. However, he was second on the regular All-Star squad and second in the Most Valuable Player voting to Abdul-Jabbar, who had been a one-man gang at L.A. But Bill never worried about awards and honors. Now he was looking forward to the playoffs.

In the first round, the Blazers had to meet the fast-finishing Chicago Bulls in a best-of-three series. Playing their usual balanced game, the Blazers won the first, lost the second, but took the third to move into the next round. It wasn't easy, but the win gave the Blazers some much needed playoff experience.

Now they moved on to a best-of-seven series against the very tough Denver Nuggets, a team that featured Bill's old college rival, David Thompson. The Nuggets also played a balanced team game. It was their first year in the NBA after coming from the ABA, and the club showed it belonged by winning the Midwest Division with a 50-32 mark. The club matched up well with the Blazers except at center, where Walton figured to outplay either Dan Issel, a good scorer, or Marvin Webster, a rebounder and shotblocker.

It's hard to call an opening game pivotal, but since Denver had the home court advantage, the Blazers wanted to win very badly. And they did, squeaking past the Nuggets, 101-100, to negate the home court factor and take a 1-0 lead in the series. Denver, however, bounced back to win the second game, also played in Denver, 121-110. In that game Bill fouled out in the fourth quarter, enabling Denver center Dan Issel to bust loose for 36 points. Bill had 19 in that one and led all rebounders with 16 caroms.

The scene shifted to Portland for game three. As usual the Blazers were red-hot on their home court. They took an early lead and hung on to win, 110-106. They then grabbed a 3-1 lead by winning game four, 105-95, once again showing a balanced attack. Denver stayed alive by winning game five in Denver, 114-105, in overtime. Now the scene shifted back to Portland for game six.

This one the Blazers blew open early.

With Bill controlling the boards and triggering the fast break, Portland raced to a 33-16 first-quarter lead and were never headed. Rookie Johnny Davis and fellow guard Lionel Hollins led the scoring with 25 and 21 respectively. Portland eliminated Denver and moved into the Western Division finals against the Lakers.

The Lakers, of course, now featured Kareem Abdul-Jabbar in the middle, and the press began making it a battle of the big men, Walton against Abdul-Jabbar. But Bill refused to get drawn into that kind of thing. "I told you I'd rather not talk about Kareem," Bill snapped at one reporter. "All I'll say is he's playing the best basketball of his life and I have to play well for us to do well against them. But as far as saying what my plans are, what kind of strategy is that?" Coach Ramsay did have an answer when asked about the two. "I like my own player," he said. "Kareem is superb; he makes their other players better. But Bill's performance is straight across the board. He doesn't have to get 40 for us to win; he can get 15 as long as he distributes the ball."

The Lakers were coming off a hard-fought seven-game series against Golden State and were tired. In fact, they asked NBA officials for a one-day postponement of game one, but there were television commitments, and the network wouldn't back off.

In the first game at L.A. the Lakers played like a tired team. Portland ran them into the floor, taking a 61-43 half-time lead and coasting home with a 121-109 win. Bill was one of four Portland players with more than 20 points, and he added 13 rebounds. As usual, he was the key man on the Portland fast break, picking up six assists with his deft passes.

Game two, also in Los Angeles, was a lot closer. In fact, at half-time Portland led by just a 54-51 count. Abdul-Jabbar was keeping the Lakers alive with his unstoppable sky hook and fine all-around play. It stayed that way right down to the wire. L.A. had a third-quarter lead, but the Blazers, led by Herm Gilliam, came back and nipped the Lakers at the end, 99-97, to go two up. Abdul-Jabbar had 40 big points, but Bill held his own even on the boards as they got 17 rebounds apiece.

The scene shifted to Portland for game three. Once again the two teams battled each other evenly. The Lakers held a 75-73 lead going into the final period. That's when Bill took over. He scored 14 of his 22 points in the last quarter, leading the Blazers on a 10-0 spurt early in the period that put them in the lead and enabled them to hang on for a 102-97 victory. Nearly everyone praised Bill's play in that one. Maurice Lucas said, "If Kareem is the best, what does that make Bill?" And Lionel Hollins added, "He did it all tonight and he wasn't even feeling well. The flu bug's been at him." They had a big

3-0 lead. One more win and they'd be in the finals.

Game four was also in Portland. Though the thought of a sweep had been improbable before, the Blazers were now on the brink. Portland took the early lead, but the Lakers kept chipping away. Yet just when they seemed ready to overtake the Blazers, another Portland player would make a big basket. Lucas was having a great offensive game, as were Davis, Hollins, and Walton. The Blazers just had too many guns, and a 30-point effort by Kareem couldn't silence them. Portland won, 105-101. They were in the finals.

"I don't think anyone has played Kareem as well as Bill has in this four-game series," said Ramsay. "I know there was that 40-point night in Los Angeles, but without Bill we couldn't have done it, even as well as everybody played."

The Blazers' opponents in the finals were the Philadelphia 76ers, a one-on-one team built around three great scorers: forwards Julius Erving and George McGinnis and guard Doug Collins. The Sixers had been under fire all year for having too many stars and not enough team play. So the final was being billed as the schoolyard players against the complete team.

For the third straight time Portland had to give up the home court advantage. Only this time they didn't get it back by winning the opener. Philly played well and hung on for a 107-101 victory. Erving and Collins led the Sixers with 33 and 30 points. They needed it because Bill had an outstanding game with 28 points and 20 big rebounds. The problem was 34 Portland turnovers that led to 26 Sixer points. Perhaps they could correct the problem in game two.

But it wasn't to be. This game was marred by a brawl featuring Philly's kid center, Darryl Dawkins, and Maurice Lucas. Both were ejected. And when the game ended, Philly had won easily, 107-89, and the experts were wondering if the Blazers could possibly come back. Julius Erving said that people were wrong in thinking a well-drilled team could pick the Sixers apart. But Herm Gilliam answered that the Blazers weren't playing their usual team game; instead they were going Philly's route and playing one on one. Game three in Portland would tell more of the story.

Back in Portland the Blazers seemed more confident. Right from the start they went to their patterned offense, working and cutting off their big man, Bill Walton. And Bill was threading the needle with his passes. Time and again he'd hit a man going down the middle for an easy lay-up. The Blazers were making it look like kid stuff and the fans loved it.

Portland opened a 34-21 first quarter lead, held it at 60-53 by the half. Philly cut the lead to five after three quarters, but then the Blazers broke loose in the fourth, led by their front line of Lucas, Walton, and Gross. When the smoke cleared, Portland had an easy 129-107 victory. They were back in it. Bill once again controlled the backboards with 18 rebounds, and his 20 points complemented Lucas' 27, Gross's 19, and Davis' 18.

But two great plays by Bill at the start of the fourth period were perhaps the keys to the win. Hollins threw a long, high, lob pass over the basket. Leaping high in the air, Bill tipped the ball in off-balance before toppling over backwards. On the inbounds play, guard Dave Twardzik stole the ball. Bill reacted instinctively and broke back toward the hoop. Twardzik lofted a high pass toward the rim. Bill went up again, caught the ball in mid-air, and slammed it through the hoop. That seemed to ignite the Blazers to their final surge.

Now came game four. It was key. If the Sixers won they'd be sitting pretty; it was a must for Portland. The game was close in the first half, Portland holding just a 48-46 lead. But in the third period the Trail Blazers began breaking and Philly came apart at the seams. The Blazers outscored the Sixers by 20 points in that period and went on to win easily, 130-98, blowing Philly out for the second straight game. Bill was forced to the bench with five fouls in the third period, but the Blazers were so hot they kept rolling without him. Lucas had 24 points and Hollins 25 for the winners. Bill had just 12, but showed his value by leading the club with seven assists, four blocked shots, and 13 rebounds.

The fifth game was back in Philly and a big one. To win the series, Portland had to win one on the Philly floor. The game followed the previous pattern: close in the first half, then Portland's fine team play and fast break opening it up in the third. By the time Philly battled back it was too late. Bill scrubbed the boards for 24 rebounds, as the Philly centers couldn't handle him. And the Portland team effort offset a brilliant 37-point performance by Erving. Portland upset the Sixers, 110-104, for their third straight win. They were now on the brink of the world championship.

Game six was back in Portland. Could the Blazers make it four straight? As Maurice Lucas said, "If Philly wants the title now, they're going to have to take it from us." Portland was confident, especially back on their home floor in front of their rabid fans. Blazermania had swept the city.

This game was a battle all the way. It was tied at 27 after one. Portland had a great second quarter and moved ahead by 12 at the half, 67-55. But the Sixers battled back. Erving was playing another super game, and McGinnis had shaken his shooting slump and was also scoring well. Yet Bill was there to grab the key rebounds and was passing brilliantly to his teammates.

With 2:20 left, Philly still trailed by eight. But Erving hit a pair of baskets, and

Lloyd Free hit a foul to reduce the lead to three. Lucas made it four with a foul shot with 1:09 remaining. Then McGinnis cut it to 109-107 with just 18 seconds to go. Portland tried to hold the ball, but McGinnis tied up Gross for a jump ball. It went to Philly.

Erving got the ball out front and went up with a 20-footer. It missed, but Philly still had the ball. Finally it came to McGinnis for a last shot. He tried a 15-footer. It was short! Bill deflected the ball to Hollins, and the clock ran out. The Blazers were champions.

Bill had been brilliant again. He had 20 points and 23 rebounds in the final, plus seven more assists and his usual handful of blocked shots. Shortly after the game ended, Bill was named the playoffs' Most Valuable Player by *Sport* magazine. No one argued with the choice. "This was better even than at UCLA," Bill cooed in the locker room. "This championship involves all the best players in the country, playing in one league. With the merger, it's truly the first championship of all the United States. And we won the first one like it."

The Blazers were brilliant, no doubt about it. They proved once more that team basketball beats one-on-one ball any day of the week. And they're a young team, averaging only 23 years of age. If they stick together and continue to play unselfishly, they could stay on top for a long time.

As for Bill, the questions have finally been

answered. It took three long, agonizing years, but he finally showed the world what people thought he'd show when he came out of UCLA: that he's truly one of the great centers of the game. Gene Shue, the Sixer coach, called him "the best basketball player for a big man in the history of the game."

That's an accurate description. It doesn't say that Bill is the best center ever. Not yet. The consensus seems to be this. He doesn't play defense quite as well as Russell. He doesn't rebound quite as well as Chamberlain. He doesn't score quite as well as Abdul-Jabbar. But he passes better than any of them and perhaps blocks shots as well. And he's so close in the other departments that he can easily become the best all-around center the game has known. But he has to stay healthy and do it over a period of time.

But don't worry, folks, Bill Walton hasn't really changed. Sure, he might have cut his long hair before the Sixer series and looks rather like the all-American boy again. But during the Blazers' victory parade in Portland, Bill showed up riding a bicycle. The sea of people engulfed him and he lost his bike. He only laughed about it, saying "it might have been the stupidest thing I've ever done." Then he added: "This is the most fun I've ever had in any sport since I started playing when I was eight years old."

About a week or so later Bill was due in New York to pick up his award (a car) from *Sport* as the playoff MVP. Word came from Portland that he couldn't make it, however, so several of his teammates went to get it instead.

And where was Bill Walton, supercenter, basketball player supreme? Why he was somewhere in Oregon, traveling down a river by raft!

★ DAVID THOMPSON ★

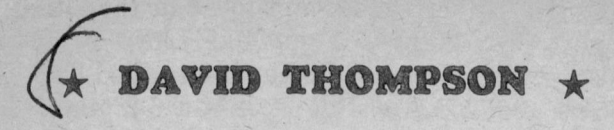

★ There was a time when it was thought that only birds could fly without the aid of modern man's machinery. But in the fall of 1972, basketball fans around the country quickly learned that the birds had company. For the first time in their lives, they saw a man fly. He didn't migrate hundreds of miles to the south for the winter. He was content with flying up, over, and around a ten-foot-high basketball rim. That's where he liked to do his flying, because he knew the solo flights paid off . . . in points and victories.

This flyer had no wings. He was a rather gentle-looking flyer, a slim, 6-4 forward. Now, a flying forward is a rare breed. This one could be identified by his markings, a red or white jersey with the word "STATE" lettered across the front. And under the lettering was the number "44." When you looked up the markings in North Carolina State's flying guide, you learned the breed was called David Thompson, and he was the only one of his kind anywhere in existence.

OK, enough of the cute stuff. So David Thompson is a guy who can jump. Right? Wrong! He doesn't jump. He soars. Sure, there are other basketball players who get up there. No one will deny Julius Erving's great leaping ability. But the Doctor is 6-7 and you rather expect him to be in the altitude. Then there is a guy like Lloyd Free, also with the 76ers, who has been called The Prince of Mid Air. But Free is a 6-2 guard and does most of his work on the outside.

David Thompson is different. He does much of his leaping around the basket. And looking at his slender 6-4 frame, his calm, almost placid face, it is an even greater shock when he takes off, soars high above the basket, hangs in the air, and slams an alley-oop pass through the hoop. David's vertical jump has been measured at 42 inches. That's more than a yard off the ground! Just get a ruler, see how high that is, and you'll know why David Thompson can fly like a bird.

But if that were all David can do, he might be a high jumper instead of an all-pro basketball star. David was one of the greatest college performers of all time, leading North Carolina State to one unbeaten season and a single-loss campaign in which they won the national championship. He also had the character, integrity, and self-assurance to say no to a two-million-dollar pro offer that would have deprived him of his final year of college. And once in the pros he performed brilliantly, living up to all expectations, first in the ABA, then in the NBA after the merger. And he's done it for his team, the Denver Nuggets, at two positions, guard and forward, swinging back and forth with ease, playing wherever it will best help his team.

In today's world of egocentric, greedy athletes who'd rather spend their days taking all they can out of the till, David Thompson is one of the rare exceptions. He's a gentleman, a player who loves the game and believes he owes something to it, to the fans who come to see him play. He'll sign autographs endlessly for hordes of admiring youngsters, always with a smile on his face, a friendly word on his lips. David Thompson is one of the few top pro athletes with no enemies. Everyone likes and respects him. It's always been that way.

David was born on July 13, 1954, in Shelby, North Carolina, and grew up in nearby Boiling Springs. He had plenty of company as a youngster. He was the last of 11 children born to Vellie and Ida Thompson, hardworking people who tried to give all their children the best they could and teach them about the ways of the world.

There was a time in the early days when David did things like swimming in the stream behind his house or fishing for catfish. Then when he was seven, he noticed his older brother, 14-year-old Vellie, Jr., doing something interesting in the backyard. He was practicing set shots at the hoop they'd just put up. From then on, basketball was the name of the game for David Thompson. Soon he was playing every chance he had. David says he learned not to blow shots at an early age, because every time he did Vellie needled continually. So David played and played, first with his brothers, then with his friends.

His father was a religious man, a deacon in the Baptist Church, and he often talked long and seriously to his children, telling them things they should know when they were ready to go out in the world. "My Dad told me that the way people acted was totally different from the way they talked," recalls David. "I'd go to Bible School and he'd teach, 'Love your brother,' and all that. So I couldn't conceive of people hating me because of the color of my skin. That was hard for me to take, but it was there. It definitely was there."

Things were changing in David's area of North Carolina. A brand-new high school was under construction, and it would take both black and white students. When David entered Crest High School, he came from one of two black junior highs and was mixed in with boys and girls from three white junior highs. The basketball coach was a man named Ed Peeler, and David remembers him well.

"Ed Peeler did a lot for getting black guys involved in athletics," says David. "If you had the ability to play, Ed made sure you played, no matter if you were black or white. I think because of that, and other reasons, things began getting better. A lot of the white kids in school had never really known a black person before, you know, on a personal basis as friends. And it was the same with the black kids. But there was no real trouble and a lot of guys with different backgrounds became friends."

Basketball was the common denominator for some of them, and for David it was quickly becoming a way of life. One of his teammates at Crest, Carl Clayton, remembers many occasions when David called up Coach Peeler in the evening to get the key to the gym. The games went on way past midnight, David always wanting to play one more, one more. Other times, when they couldn't use the gym, they went over to nearby Gardner-Webb College, and worked out there. It was all basketball for David then, though he was a good student as well.

Once he began playing for Crest High, it was obvious that he was no ordinary ballplayer. David was a worker; he already had his fantastic leaping ability along with the knowledge to use it to his advantage. In fact, during the early days of his Crest career, he was seen by Larry Brown, who was a pro guard at the time and who would later be David's coach at Denver. At any rate, Brown saw him and came away awestruck. He immediately contacted his former coach, Dean Smith of North Carolina University. "Coach," said Brown excitedly. "I saw something last night I couldn't believe, a fourteen-and-a-half year old who's the most talented young kid I've ever seen play. He's got a flair about him that separates him from even the great players."

Another important person in David's life to see him way back then was Carl Scheer. Scheer was a lawyer at that time, but someone who also loved basketball and wanted to get involved in the pro game. He did. As president and general manager of the Denver Nuggets, he would later sign David to his first pro contract. But after seeing David play as a young high schooler, Scheer said: "This kind of performer comes along once every hundred years!" From then on, Scheer was another one who followed every single phase of David's career, watching the youngster progress from high school star to college superstar and living for the day when he could have a shot at signing him as a pro.

David continued to spark the Crest team for three years. In his senior year the team took 28 straight wins, then lost the last game of the season. After that David played in the All-Star Game, the Marion North Carolina Civitan Classic. It was an exciting contest, with some of the best ballplayers in the area involved. And with seconds remaining, David's team was down a point, and one of his teammates was on the foul line with a chance to tie the game.

David lined up outside the lane. The shot was up ... and off the rim, bouncing off to the side opposite David. But with a quick movement, he leaped high in the air and across the width of the foul lane, stayed in the air, and tapped the rebound back in for the winning score. It was an unbelievable play, one that witnesses will never forget. One of those who watched the game was Crest's principal, Edward Clayton, the father of David's friend, Carl Clayton. "I always said that David's timing was a little bit off on that play," says Mr. Clayton. "Of course he made the winning basket, but when he came down to the floor there were still two seconds left on the clock. Had his timing been right, he would have stayed up in the air until the clock had run out!"

That was, of course, intended as a joke. But it also showed the tremendous respect and reverence with which David was regarded during his high school years. There were people who really believed that David could hang in the air as long as he liked. And sometimes it seemed as if he was up there forever.

But back down on earth David had to go about the business of choosing a college. Plenty of schools wanted him, but he more or less wanted to stay close to home. And everyone knew you could play big-time basketball in North Carolina, what with North Carolina University, North Carolina State, Duke, and others.

Dean Smith at North Carolina remembered Larry Brown's enthusiastic phone call of several years back, and he also witnessed David's play. He'd be crazy not to want the 6-4 forward. And he tried . . . tried hard. David listened as he listened carefully to all those who wanted to recruit him, including

Norm Sloan of North Carolina State. And it was N.C. State that David eventually chose. "The year before I got there," David says, "State signed a lot of other good young ballplayers. I felt my chances of winning a national championship would be better there. Plus I visited the campus and met some of the other players and really felt comfortable there."

So David packed off to Raleigh, North Carolina, in the fall of 1971, ready to start his first year at North Carolina State University. When basketball season started, David reported to the freshman team with his usual zest and zeal and willingness to work long and hard. While not a hollar-type guy, he was nevertheless a leader by example, a player who would do anything for the good of the team.

He was a standout for the freshman team right from the beginning. In fact, he was a spectacular player, his soaring leaps into the higher regions of the arena garnering screams of disbelief from the fans. Many fans began coming out to the home games early just to see the freshman play. They were already drooling with dreams of national glory when David joined the varsity the next season.

The varsity, with those good young players David mentioned, compiled a fine 16-10 record. They seemed a player or two away from a big year. And as for David, he tore up the freshman league, scoring 569 points in 16 games for a sensational 35.6 average. He hit on 55.4 percent of his shots, averaged 13.6 rebounds a game, and had a high game of 54 points. He was all the Wolfpack had hoped for ... and more.

In the fall of 1972-73, David joined the varsity. Also coming up from that fine freshman team was 5-7 guard Monte Towe. Towe was a little guy, but a pugnacious competitor and a great floor leader in the backcourt. He earned a starting job right off the bat. Also coming to the varsity were guard Morris "Mo" Rivers and forward Tim Stoddard, a 6-8 rebounder. Both these players would also contribute heavily in the upcoming years. They joined an already solid cast let by 7-4 center Tom Burleson. Burleson was tall and thin and, in some people's minds, lacking in certain talents. In other words, he was no Bill Walton. But he had a good shot, worked very hard, and was a gutty player. Despite his limitations, he was a leader and could be counted on in the tough games. The team was one of multi-talented players and seemingly unlimited potential.

For a brief period before the year began, there was some fear that the club wouldn't have David after all. He was so impressive as a freshman that the Kentucky Colonels of the ABA made some overtures toward him. They were willing to sign him right after his freshman year, but David would have no part of that. "I had my goals when I came to N.C. State," David explained. "I wanted to play on a national championship team and I wanted to earn my degree. That was very important to me. You see a lot of players go to college for four years and not graduate, then play pro ball three or four years, and what do they have left after that?"

There were always people who said David was crazy to turn down million-dollar offers to stay at college. After all, you never know what might happen, and suddenly the money might not be there. But once he got to know David, Coach Norm Sloan explained it easily. "Maybe you and I can't understand it," Coach Sloan said. "But remember, many of us today are frightened people. David was an excellent student. He wanted a degree and he was very sure of his ability. Most people who give up eligibility to sign aren't very good students and probably won't graduate anyhow. In addition, they're unsure of themselves. They say, 'That money is here this year; it might not be next year.' That's the way the average person thinks. But David would say repeatedly. 'If that money is there this year, it'll be there next year.' That was his attitude toward it—and there aren't many men who have that kind of confidence."

There was another problem in 1972-73. The Wolfpack were on probation by the NCAA for some alleged recruiting violations and therefore ineligible for any postseason tournaments. So the club wanted to prove its worth during the regular season. They opened up against some lesser teams and immediately showed the basketball world that they had incredible firepower. Playing the likes of Appalachian State, Atlantic Christian, Georgia Southern, and South Florida, they won their games by scores of 130-53, 110-40, 144-100, and 125-88.

Some people began talking about the club as a new basketball powerhouse, while others said they were simply taking advantage of powder puff schools. But there was no denying what the team had going for it. Thompson was playing outstanding basketball, shooting and rebounding well, and already showing his flair for the spectacular. He and Towe were starting to work their alley-oops. David would run underneath, leap high in the air well over the rim. Towe would then loft a pass that David would grab at the top of his jump and slam home. It was a great crowd pleaser and an effective scoring play.

In addition, Burleson and the rest of the team were playing well, and the four relatively easy games gave them a chance to put it together as a team. But now the picnic was over. They'd be starting to go against the other Atlantic Coast Conference teams, and the brand of ball in the ACC was as good as anywhere, the rivalries as intense. There is always tremendous competition between North Carolina, N.C. State, Duke, Maryland, Wake Forest, Clemson, and Virginia.

But the Wolfpack quickly showed they

were for real. Playing in the Big 4 Tournament, they defeated Wake Forest, 88-83, and then North Carolina, 68-61. The scores indicate just how intense the rivalry in the ACC can be. The scores are usually close, and weaker teams often pull off upsets when riding an emotional high.

Following the tourney, N.C. State whipped Davidson, Georgia, Virginia, Duke, and Lehigh. They had won 10 straight games and were now ranked number three in the country. The number two team was ACC rival Maryland, also unbeaten and featuring some fine players of its own, notably big men Tom McMillen and Len Elmore. By the way, the top team in the country was UCLA, led by junior center Bill Walton.

The first confrontation between the Wolfpack and the Terrepins was ready to begin. Maryland and its volatile coach, Lefty Driesell, made no bones about their ambition. They wanted the national championship and didn't intend to let N.C. State stand in their way. The game was being played at Maryland's home court at College Park, so they figured to have the advantage with a packed house of screaming, partisan fans.

Maryland was a slight favorite for another reason. Towe was coming in with a recently broken nose and would be wearing a special face mask. The little guard, who had been playing very well, also had his left wrist in a plastic splint to protect a broken bone. And if that wasn't enough, he had a pinched nerve in his leg. The Pack needed a healthy Towe to run their backcourt. As Coach Sloan said, "Monte has character leapin' out of him. He really takes his lumps, but he takes charge, too. When he talks out there, everybody listens."

David had started the season like gangbusters. In fact, after those early season slaughters of the weak teams, he was actually leading the country in scoring and getting nationwide press reviews. But David had tapered off. His scoring average had dipped under 30, and he seemed to be coming back to earth. Some people were beginning to say he wasn't as good as all that. But David himself made it sound as if he came right out of the comic books, à la Plastic Man. "Sometimes I go up to block a shot and I feel like the ball is just a little out of my reach," he said. "Then it seems like I can feel my arm growing. It's coming right out of my shoulder. And all of a sudden I can stretch and reach the ball."

As usual, the two teams battled hard. Maryland tried to use a zone press during the first half, but with Towe playing well despite his injuries, the Wolfpack penetrated and scored. At the half State had moved in front, 53-44. The Maryland abandoned the zone press at the outset of the second half and fought back. There was no denying that the Terps had a fine team, and their sharpshooters began to offset a brilliant game by

David, who was scoring both outside and inside.

Finally the Terps tied it, and with four minutes left they took an 85-83 lead. The Wolfpack advantage was gone; Maryland seemed to have the momentum. But then Coach Dreisell may have made a mistake. He ordered the Terps to stall, to hold the ball instead of pursuing their advantage. The clock continued to wind down. Then State got the ball back, scored, and tied it at 85.

That was still the score with 1:45 left. Maryland had the ball and fed it into McMillen, who tried a long hook shot and missed. Burleson got the rebound for State. The Wolfpack then ran the clock down to 12 seconds. They didn't have a set play, and big Burleson wound up with the ball. But he was some 25 feet from the hoop. With the clock running out he shot. The ball went off the rim.

"I had faked and broken to the inside and was open," said David, reliving the play. "But Burleson didn't see me and took the shot. I had position on the boards and just went up. The ball was there." And when ball and David come together the result is generally a basket. This time it was a winning basket, and David's 37th point of the game. The Pack had won it, 87-85. David had silenced any remaining critics and so had the Wolfpack. There was little doubt now that they were a top team. In fact, they assumed the number two spot in the weekly polls behind UCLA and stayed there.

Coach Sloan and his players knew they couldn't be in the NCAA playoffs, so they had to give it their best shot during the season. They kept winning. They beat Maryland again, 89-78, and continued to roll—their closest game an 82-78 victory over Wake Forest. When the regular season ended, the Wolfpack were still unbeaten with a 25-0 slate. And although they couldn't go to the NCAA tournament, they could still play for the ACC title.

Once again they came through, beating Virginia, 63-51, and then topping Maryland for a third time in another brutal battle, 76-74. It was the greatest season in N.C. State history, 27-0, but the Wolfpack couldn't prove they were number one. They wouldn't get a chance to meet UCLA.

David was far and away the best sophomore in the nation—many thought already the best player. In 27 games he scored 666 points for a 24.7 average, with a high game of 40. He had a shooting percentage of 56.9 and grabbed 8.1 rebounds a game. He was a unanimous first team all-America selection in all the major polls. It would be hard to imagine a better sophomore season.

Then David settled down to his studies and practicing more basketball. The team would be off probation the following year, and with all the key players back, it would be their best chance at the national championship. In addition, UCLA and Bill Walton were on the regular season schedule. It promised to be an exciting year, one all the players were looking forward to.

Before the 1973-74 season began, David went in to see Coach Sloan. He had heard that the school had discontinued the junior varsity program that year. David wanted to know how many players would be traveling with the team. The coach said about 12.

"What about the rest of the guys?" David asked.

"Well," answered Sloan, "you aren't suggesting we dress all 17 people, are you?"

"Is there a rule against it?" asked David.

Looking back at the incident, Sloan said. "The amazing part about it is here is a guy who is the best college player in the country, the very best, a guy who's probably gonna get a couple of million dollars from the pros, and he's concerned about the other end of the bench. All I can say is that's David."

On the court David and his teammates started right where they left off, whipping East Carolina and Vermont by big scores. But this time game three wouldn't be a cakewalk. It was against defending national champ UCLA. The Game was played at a neutral court in St. Louis.

Well, it wasn't really much of a game. The Bruins had a good night and the Wolfpack didn't. Walton was dominating the boards, and the UCLA defense was giving David and his mates a tough time. The Bruins took an early lead and held it, building slowly and confidently to an 84-66 win—a decisive margin of victory. It stopped the Wolfpack winning streak at 29 games and also re-established UCLA as the nation's number one team: the team to beat at the season's end. "It was a real whippin' we gave them," said one UCLA player. And the Bruins wily coach, John Wooden, said simply, "I want State to dwell on that 18-point margin." It was as if Wooden sensed that they would be meeting again.

The Wolfpack were bitterly disappointed. David had just 17 points against the Bruins, Burleson just 11, Towe 14. But forward Tim Stoddard served as a spokesman for the team. "We know they aren't 18 points better than us," he said. "But what's more important is that *they* know it." In just the third game of the season the psychological warfare was building for the season's end. But first things first. The Pack had to get back on the track.

And they did. They whipped Georgia, then won the Sugar Bowl Tournament by defeating Villanova and Memphis State. They repeated in the Big 4 Tourney by taking North Carolina in a squeaker, 78-77, and Wake Forest, 91-73. And after beating Clemson, they met arch-rival Maryland once more.

The game was David's from the beginning. He was on and he went to work, hitting jumpers from out front and the side, moving underneath for lay-ups and rebounds. And more than once he brought the crowd to its feet with a spectacular alley-oop slam-dunk. When it ended, David had 41 points and N.C. State had an 80-74 win.

After that the Pack continued to roll, beating Maryland again and everyone else in their path. In fact, there were no real scares the rest of the way. They finished the season with a 24-1 record and were right behind UCLA in the national rankings.

David had some more big games—games of 39, 40, 35—but he was a team player who wanted to see balanced scoring and everybody happy. He never gunned or worried about his own stats. His next concern was helping his team get through the ACC tournament.

The Pack took Virginia easily in the first game, 87-66, with David ramming home 37 points. But in the title game against Maryland it was another war, another battle in what had become the number one rivalry in the land. State had taken the Terps five straight times in two years, and Dreisell's charges were sky-high. The lead changed hands time and again as the two teams battled all out for the right to go to the NCAA playoffs.

At the end of regulation play it was tied, and out they went again for another five minutes. Finally the firepower of N.C. State prevailed. The Pack won it, 103-100. They were ACC champs once more and off to the national championships. In the Maryland game Burleson had the greatest game of his career with 38 points, and David was right behind with 29. It was a great victory, but there were more to come.

In the Eastern Regionals, State defeated Providence, 92-78, with David racking up 40 points. Then came the Regional final against the University of Pittsburgh. State leaped out to an early lead and seemed ready to romp. Then, midway through the first half, David charged across the lane toward the hoop and went up for an alley-oop. One of the Pitt defenders, operating far below, hit David's legs, inadvertently upending him. That was a constant fear of his coaches and mates when he went up so high. He did a cartwheel and came down hard ... head first. He lay motionless, and the huge crowd fell silent.

David was unconscious for several minutes. When he finally came to, he was helped from the court and to the hospital for an examination. The Wolfpack players and fans hoped he was all right, not only because he was the key to the title, but also because he was so well-liked.

With David at the hospital, the team pulled together and continued to roll, playing inspired ball, a win-it-for-David kind of thing. Then, with about five minutes left, David suddenly reappeared and walked slowly to the State bench. His head was wrapped in a white bandage to cover 15 stitches needed to close a gash. But there was no fracture and only a mild concussion. The fans rose and gave David a standing ovation. He then sat and watched his team make it into the final round of four with a 100-72 victory. David had just eight points when he left, but Burleson ended with 26, Towe with 19, guard Mo Rivers with 17. The others had picked up the slack.

Now the club would face UCLA in the semifinals. This was the one they wanted. And it would be played in Greensboro, North Carolina, so the crowd would be on their side. The Bruins were hoping the Wolfpack remembered that 18-point loss early in the season. But the State players remembered it in only a positive way. They felt they were a much improved team, in fact, a better all-around team than the Bruins.

During the first half it was a close game, both teams being careful not to make any errors. One would get the lead, then the other would catch up. N.C. State fans were relieved to see David moving and performing well, showing no ill effects from his collision with the floor a week earlier. And he wasn't at all gun-shy, still operating in the upper reaches whenever the situation called for it. But it was an even match in the first half, and when the two clubs left the floor at half-time, it was all tied at 35.

Then, early in the second half, UCLA began to spurt. They rolled it up to 49-38, an 11-point bulge, and people were reminded of the game early in the year when the Bruins put it away. And it could have happened again. Then Burleson, who was having a fine game, made a key play. It began when State missed another shot, and Walton grabbed the rebound. If the Bruins broke and scored the lead would be up to 13. But as Walton held the ball over his head looking for an outlet, Burleson reached in from behind, cleanly swept the ball from Walton's hands, and put it in the basket. The Pack then staged a brief rally. But minutes later UCLA took control again, and with 11 minutes to go they had build up another 11-point margin, this one at 57-46.

Once again the fans were quiet. But they came to life as the Pack rolled back again. Little Towe sped past the UCLA defenders and then fed David or Burleson underneath. N.C. State reeled off 10 straight points and were right back in the ball game once more. This time they stayed close. They drew within one at 61-60.

Then David cut toward the hoop, went a mile high, took a Towe pass at the top of his leap, and put it through. In addition, he was fouled and made the shot, giving State the lead for the first time since the first half, 63-61. Now it was a battle, a grim, classic battle between the best two college teams in the land.

With just 51 seconds left the score was tied at 65. The Bruins had the ball and went into Walton, who missed a hook shot. Burleson got the boards and State had the ball. They held for one last, good shot. But none of their scorers could get loose, and Tim Stoddard had the ball with five seconds left. He tried a shot from the corner and missed. The buzzer sounded and the game went into overtime.

Both teams were tentative in the overtime period, each scoring one basket. State finally got the ball when Stoddard stole it from Greg Lee. Then they held it again. With 10 seconds left David drove for the hoop. But he decided to pass off to Burleson instead of shooting, and the big center missed. Once again the buzzer sounded and now was a second overtime. This time the two teams let it out. Both began running and shooting, UCLA having the better of it. With 3:27 left they had taken a 74-67 lead. Could the Wolfpack possibly come back again?

They did. They tightened it up defensively and began to close the gap. The lead was five, then three, then one. With a little more than a minute left, David hit a jumper over Keith Wilkes, putting the Pack ahead, 76-75. Seconds later Wilkes pushed David, and the two successful free throws made it 78-75. Suddenly, State was taking control.

With just 27 seconds left Burleson stole a pass, got to ball to Towe, and Monte was fouled. His free throws made it 80-75, and that just about sewed it up. A last-second basket by Walton didn't change the result. The Pack had won the biggest victory in their history. They had turned defeat into victory and, after two years, had proved that they deserved to be number one. David led the way with 28 points and 10 rebounds. Burleson also played a great game, scoring 20 and grabbing 14 rebounds, while Towe chipped in with 12 and played a great floor game. All this negated Walton's 29 points and 18 rebounds.

The Pack still had to prepare for one more showdown. It was only the semifinals; they weren't national champions yet. They still had to play Al McGuire's Marquette Warriors, a tough, well-disciplined, ball-control team. It wouldn't be easy.

It wasn't. During the first half the Marquette slowdown and patience kept the Pack off-balance. Late in the period Marquette took a 28-27 lead. But a technical foul, a pair of free throws by David, a hoop by Burleson, and a goaltending call all combined to help State to a 39-30 half-time lead. After that it was a matter of time. At one point in the second half State led by 19, and they cruised home with a 76-64 win. They were national champions! David had again led a balanced scoring attack with 21 points.

What an incredible year it had been. David, of course, was all-everything. Among his many honors were unanimous first-team all-America everywhere and college basketball's Player of the Year. He averaged 26 points a game, but again played an unselfish, team oriented style.

Tom Burleson was graduating from the 1973-74 team, and although David, Towe, Mo Rivers, and a few others would be back, there really wasn't anyone to replace the big center. The team would undoubtedly be a big winner again, but, without that big seven-footer in the middle, it was unlikely they could repeat their great triumphs of the past year. Knowing that, some pro teams again began scheming to get David. They figured he had reached the pinnacle and would just be playing out the string as a senior. Now would be a good time to nail him.

But once again David said no to any and all overtures. He still wanted to finish school and get his degree. And he felt he owed something to his teammates and the many fans who expected him back. That's the kind of guy he is. Coach Sloan, in fact, would talk about David's character every chance he had. "David is without question the finest athlete I have ever coached," said the coach. "His athletic skills are just unbelievable as far as strength, speed, coordination, jumping ability. But the thing that really impresses me so much is that David is a finer person than he is an athlete, if you can believe it. Over the years I've observed that all too often great athletes are abrasive-type personalities. They rub people the wrong way. David's greatest fans are his own teammates."

The coach then talked about his star's relationship to the game of basketball and the way he looks at it. "David loves basketball. It's his life. And he's found a way to relax and let loose all the talent within him. He has a good brain and his self-confidence and he has self-respect because of the way he has lived his life. Very few of us have that clean an opinion of ourselves. So many of us have cheated along the way, compromised with life, and David has never done that. He's just kind of gone out and done the right thing and therefore he isn't burdened with the guilt feelings that a lot of people have."

So David was back for another year. The Pack had to rebuild its offense because they didn't really have a big man. But any team with David Thompson is going to be formidable. The team surprised everyone by winning their first eight games. Some were relatively easy, but they did take Virginia, Oregon State, Davidson, and Pittsburgh in the spurt—all good teams.

Of necessity, David was doing more offensively now, playing some 33-, 42-, 57-, 43-, and 39-point games in the early going. The 57 points came against Buffalo, as the Pack ran up 144 points. But the club came back to earth in the Big 4 Tourney, losing to Wake Forest, 83-78, David having a bad game with only 15. Three games later Maryland finally broke the jinx and beat them, 103-88. Yet, though the Pack was no longer an overpowering team, they were still a good one and in the top ten most of the year.

There were other losses: another to Maryland, one to Clemson, and one to North Carolina. But the Pack still had a shot at the ACC title and NCAA playoffs. First they beat Virginia, 91-85, with David canning 38 points. Then came the big one, an 87-85 upset of Maryland. David got 30 points, the victory put the Pack in the finals. But the Tar Heels of North Carolina were a power again and they beat State for the second time (State had also beaten them twice), this one the title game, 70-66. And David closed out his college career with just a 16-point effort.

But it hadn't been the lost season some people were predicting. The Pack finished with a 22-6 record and were ranked number seven in the country. As for David, he scored 838 points in 28 games for a 29.9 average. That gave him a school record of 2,309 points and a 26.8 mark for his career. Needless to say, he was all-everything again, including Player of the Year, and the most desirable player to enter the pro ranks at forward in quite some time.

Of course David didn't just sit on his haunches and wait for the draft. He went back to studying, completed his work, and graduated with a degree in sociology. And when the draft came around he had a decision to make. The NBA and ABA were still separate and competing for available talent. There was already talk of a merger, but while the leagues were still competing, players like David could command huge contracts. But there was more to signing than money. David wanted to go where he'd be happiest, where he could fit in as part of a winning team. Then, sure enough, David found he was the number one choice of the Atlanta Hawks of the NBA and Denver Nuggets of the ABA.

Unlike other players, David didn't keep both teams on a string, didn't wait while the price went higher and higher. He just thought carefully about his choices, made his decision, and then negotiated a contract in good faith. He decided to sign with the Denver Nuggets of the ABA. "I looked at things from a perspective and thought there would be a better situation for me in Denver," says David. "For instance, I talked to John Drew [Hawks star] about Atlanta and he told me he liked it a lot, but I had to do what I thought was best for me. The team [the Hawks] wasn't that stable at the time and they were not drawing. It was a totally opposite situation in Denver.

"My whole experience was playing before big crowds since we usually had sellouts at State. And I was familiar with Coach Larry Brown. Plus the team unity on the Nuggets really caught my eye. They had some fine players and were signing others. I could see they had the making of a really good team. Therefore there'd be no pressure on me of having to turn the franchise around. That has hurt a lot of ballplayers, that kind of pressure.

"There's one other thing that I can say

now. If there was any doubt in my mind that there wouldn't have been a merger in the near future, I would never have signed with the ABA. But I felt the two leagues would have to work something out sooner or later. To be honest, it happened sooner than even I thought."

As Coach Norm Sloan had always said, David had a great deal of self-awareness and self-confidence. So when some critics charged that he had signed with the weaker league, David didn't let it bother him at all, though he did feel compelled to defend the ABA against its critics. "I didn't believe the ABA was a lesser league. The teams coming out of the ABA could compete with anybody. And any team from either league coming into Denver with the attitude that they'll dominate us will be in for a big surprise."

David knew what he was talking about; he was joining a team that already had some fine established players. At center was 6-9 Dan Issel, one of the best scorers in ABA history and still a young player at 27. The other forward opposite David was Bobby Jones, also 6-9, but lightning quick and a fine defensive and team-minded player. In the backcourt were 6-5 Ralph Simpson, an ABA All-Star and fine scorer, and playmaker Chuck Williams. The bench also showed some good depth with a blend of veterans and youngsters.

The man David would have to negotiate his first pro contract with was Carl Scheer, an admirer of many years' standing. There was no real problem ironing out a contract. Scheer knew what he was getting. But he wouldn't tell the press or media the figures involved. "Pick a number," he said, teasingly. "I'll say one thing. It's the biggest contract I ever negotiated with a player. I think I can safely say David signed for more than Jabbar when he came out of college. David is probably the highest paid rookie in pro ball this year.

"But he's worth it. We knew the kind of player he would be and felt our investment over a period of years would pay off. He's a gentleman and an extremely popular player. He's always been that way. We knew the fans would come out to see him."

It was rumored that David's contract was in the neighborhood of $3.5 million for a period of six years. Of course, in this day of complex, long-term contracts, there can be a multitude of ways the finances can be dispensed. Needless to say, David signed for big money and everyone was happy.

One other interesting event occurred. The Nuggets also signed Monte Towe, David's best friend and teammate from N.C. State. Towe, at 5-7, would be the smallest man in pro basketball, leading some people to speculate that the signing of Towe was a move to ensure the signing of Thompson. But Towe, a gritty competitor, might do well in certain spots and with certain matchups. The club also signed young center Marvin Webster, a

7-1 shotblocker and rebounder. The club was trying to build, hoping to dominate the ABA and then compete in the NBA if and when there was a merger.

It didn't take long for David to settle into his role as a starting forward. He was the team's leading scorer almost from the beginning and one of the top scorers in the ABA. In addition, the Nuggets, with a balance of talent, had the best record in the league for the entire season.

The big problem was the ABA itself. More teams were beset with financial problems and several folded as the season progressed. It was obvious that league couldn't survive on its own much longer. In fact, by the final month or so of the season, the remaining seven teams were playing in one condensed division. And talks were under way to merge the leagues in some manner the following season.

David nevertheless kept his mind on basketball. He was doing many of the same things he had done in college: hitting jump shots, driving, and using his amazing leaping ability to perform his wizardry around the rim. He was the spectacular performer Carl Scheer thought he'd be. Combined with the other Nuggets, he was helping the team to win ball games. By midseason David was one of the most popular players in the league, both as a person and as a competitor. He was averaging in the mid-20's and was among the scoring leaders.

He did admit there was some transition that had to be made.

"Because all the players in the pros are more talented than the college players, there was a certain amount of adjustment to be made on the court," David explained. "But because I'm surrounded by a great bunch of guys, the transition has not been difficult for me.

"There were also social adjustments to be made, the fact that I was on my own and had to make more major decisions. But that came, too. I feel I know basically what pro basketball is all about and I know the things I can do and the things in which I'm limited.

"My game is penetrating to the basket and opening up avenues for other players and this is what I'm trying to do. I try to give the fans their money's worth every night. But don't forget, we have so many good players that I can be terrible and we still win. It wasn't like that in college.

"So it doesn't get me down if I don't have a real good night one night, because I know I can come back the next night. You have to take those things in stride in pro basketball. Sometimes you're just flat-out tired. It just doesn't happen for you every night."

It happened enough nights for David to have a Rookie of the Year season. He helped the Nuggets to a 60-24 record and a first-place finish, some five games ahead of the New York Nets. David played in 83 games and scored 2,158 points for a 26.0 average.

He shot 51.5 percent from the field. In addition, he grabbed 525 rebounds and handed out 308 assists. His scoring made him number three in the league behind a pair of pretty good sharpshooters, Julius Erving and Billy Knight. Those same two players beat him for the forward spots on the league all-star team, though David, Bobby Jones, and Dan Issel all made the second team.

When the season was nearly over, the always candid Thompson talked about his game, the things he did and learned, and his strengths and weaknesses. "I think the main reason I can help a team so much is that I'm pretty versatile," he said. "If my opponent is applying pressure, I can bring the ball up because I'm a lot quicker than most of the forwards I play. I also like to create three-on-two situations where I can pass off for a basket or go in for the score myself. My quickness enables me to do this.

"Of course, there are disadvantages to being 6-4 and playing forward. I'm often a lot shorter than the man I'm up against. Plus I'm not a real physical ballplayer. I don't have the best body in the world and I get pushed around a lot. But I'm adjusting to it. They set some pretty ferocious picks out there and some guys come after your head. But I'm learning to sidestep them instead of trying to go through them."

Someone asked David how he would defend against himself, an obviously implausible situation. But David answered quickly,

"I'd probably try to deny me the ball. If you don't have the ball you can't do too much. Also, I would play off me, back off a step, so I couldn't beat me to the basket." Of course, David Thompson, the offensive player, would find a way to beat that, too.

But back to business. Though there was just a single, seven-team division left in the ABA, there was nevertheless a playoff, involving the first four teams. Denver went up against Kentucky in one semifinal and New York against San Antonio in the other. The Nuggets were heavy favorites to take the ABA title.

Kentucky wasn't easy. They had overwhelming board strength with Artis Gilmore and Maurice Lucas, and some deft sharpshooters. Denver won the first game, 110-107, the closeness of the score showing how tough the contest was going to be. The Colonels stormed back to take the next two, and Denver barely tied it up in the fourth game, 108-106. Then the Nuggets grabbed the fifth, only to have Kentucky take the sixth in double-overtime. But in the deciding game David, Issel, and the rest were too much for Kentucky, pouring it on for a 133-110 victory. Now they were in the finals against the Nets.

Most experts figured that the Nuggets would win. The Nets had made some trades that didn't work out too well. To many they were basically a one-man team, although that one man was capable of almost anything. He was Julius Erving. And in the six games it took the Nets to beat the Nuggets, Julius Erving put on one of the greatest displays of all-around basketball ever seen.

For example, the Nets won the first game by two points, 120-118. Erving had 45 in that one. In the second game, which Denver managed to win, 127-121, the Doctor had 49. He was unstoppable. The Nets then won the next two, putting themselves in great position. Then Denver won game five, but the Nets came on to take the sixth and the ABA title.

Erving had averaged 34.6 in his club's 13 playoff games. By comparison, David also played extremely well. In Denver's 13 games, he averaged 26.4, just over his season's average, showing the tremendous consistency he had achieved in his rookie year. He also shot 53.6 percent from the floor in the playoffs, just above his season's mark. The guy was the real thing.

In the off-season David settled down in Denver. He and his good friend Monte Towe shared a house together and helped all they could in the community, working with kids, giving clinics, and promoting the Nuggets through their friendliness and popularity. David Thompson was a happy person. "Yes, I always been pretty happy, content, and satisfied," David said. "I have the things I need now, and I'm able to help my family, which has always been important to me."

Also during that off-season, a great upheaval was occurring in professional basketball. It had been obvious for a number of years that the ABA was in bad trouble. There were some strong franchises, but also some weak ones. And because they were in a great bidding war for talent, they were spending fortunes on young players and on discontented NBA free agents. Their expenses were incredibly high. Still they had no national television contract, and that hurt. It just seemed a matter of time.

Of course, another problem was predicting what the NBA would do. They could just sit back and watch the ABA fold, then grab up the players. Or they could try to assimilate the ABA teams and enlarge their league. Finally the decision was made. The NBA would take four ABA franchises intact— New York, San Antonio, Indiana, and Denver. And the players from the other three—Kentucky, St. Louis, Virginia—would be distributed among all the teams from both leagues.

The Nuggets' moving into the NBA intact made Carl Scheer, Larry Brown, and all the players very happy. But they wanted their club to be strong and competitive, a challenger in its first NBA year. They began to make some moves. First, they sent Ralph Simpson to Detroit, figuring the big guard just couldn't fit in with the team's style of play. They also acquired forward Gus Gerard from the defunct St. Louis team. With Gerard and Jones, perhaps David could move into the backcourt and give the team stability and punch back there. The club also acquired Paul Silas, a free agent forward from the Celtics. Silas was a defensive forward and rebounder who was expected to give the club defensive punch off the bench. Veteran ABA guards Ted McClain and Roland "Fatty" Taylor were now also Nuggets.

David was really happy that things had worked out so well. Playing in the NBA had been a dream all along. "The idea of playing in the NBA, the excitement of it all," he exclaimed, "Well, it's like being a rookie all over. I'll be playing against guys I've read about ever since I was a little kid, like Kareem Abdul-Jabbar, who's such a great ballplayer. And I'll be thrilled just being on the same court with a guy like John Havlicek, one of my idols. It's going to be a real challenge."

It didn't take long for the Nuggets to prove they belonged in the NBA. With David playing at guard and the added firepower up front, the Nuggets got off fast. They won 12 of their first 15 games, not only to take the lead in their division, but to show the best record in the entire NBA. Many former ABA players were doing well in the older league, but the Nuggets were clearly the best team. San Antonio was also over .500, but the Indiana Pacers and the Nets (now without Doctor J) were struggling and would struggle all year long.

David had made the switch to guard with

relative ease. He was scoring at a 25.4 clip his first month in the NBA, once again showing the consistency that marked his college career and his rookie year in the ABA. And he already had some comments on his change of position. "I was optimistic about the switch," he said. "I felt I could adjust easily. It took me a little while to get comfortable back there, but it really hasn't affected my game much . . . I can do pretty much the same things at guard that I could at forward. A lot of our plays are interchangeable, and I can get in a few dunks, which is always a lot of fun."

An early-season game with the tough L.A. Lakers and Abdul-Jabbar showed clear evidence of the Nuggets' firepower. It was a tough, close game all the way, with the Nuggets holding a 31-29 lead at the quarter and 59-54 advantage at the half. The Lakers closed to 89-88 at the end of three, but then the Nuggets came on in the final quarter to win, 122-112.

Issel led the way for the Nuggets with 27 points. David had 25 on 10 for 17 from the floor. Bobby Jones had 20 and 18 rebounds, while Ted McClain and Paul Silas had 16 each. Paul also grabbed 10 rebounds. The team seemed well-balanced and very deep.

For a good part of the year the Nuggets continued to have the best record in the league. But in the second half, though they were still winning, they were not as overpowering as they had been earlier. One thing the club wanted was more scoring punch up front. Jones was basically a defensive and passing forward, while Gerard didn't really fill the bill. Silas also specialized in defense, while veteran Willie Wise was unable to regain his former all-ABA form.

So up came David again, and this move created a problem in the backcourt. The club had to deal again, getting Jim Price, an NBA vet, and Mack Calvin, another former ABA star. Now the team lacked a big scorer on the backline. And while Issel was an outstanding scoring center, he left a bit to be desired on defense and rebounding. But the club was well-coached and well-disciplined. There was never a chance of losing the division lead.

Late in the season the Nuggets went up against the Knicks, no longer a formidable force, but still a team with some great stars. David was off at the outset; in fact, he made just two of 10 shots in the opening half. "I told him if he stopped shooting I'd break his arms," said Coach Brown. "When you're that kind of player, your next 10 shots may all fall through."

Sure enough, David turned it around and made 11 of his next 13, finished with 30 points, and led the Nuggets to a 114-108 win—a game in which Denver came from 24 down to take it. "It was nice beating the Knicks, especially here in Madison Square Garden," David said. "And what makes it especially nice is beating another NBA team.

People know we're for real now, but it's nice to be able to keep proving it."

Coming back up to the forward position seemed to please David. For instance, that night against the Knicks he pulled down seven rebounds and was still in the action enough to hand off for seven assists. He seemed to be more valuable up front and indicated that he liked playing there better. "Yes, I like forward better than guard," he admitted. "The reason is that the other teams have to adjust to compensate for my quickness. Besides, playing guard I had to worry about bringing the ball up and playing pressure defense from baseline to baseline. I'd get tired and it would hurt my offense. In a tough game like this one I felt relaxed because I was at forward and I didn't have as much to worry about."

As usual, David was being completely candid and honest. He helped rally his team to a 50-32 finish, best in their division. And in their first year in the NBA, the Nuggets tied Philadelphia for the second best record in the league. L.A. was tops with a 53-29 log. Now Denver would have a bye in the first round of the playoffs, and would have to get ready to meet the winner of the Chicago-Portland series.

David finished fourth in the entire NBA in scoring, behind Maravich, Billy Knight, and Abdul-Jabbar. Fast company. He scored 2,152 points in 82 games, a 25.9 average. What consistency. As a rookie in the ABA he averaged 26.0. David was again a better than 50 percent shooter, and he led the Nuggets in assists with 337, despite being shifted between the backcourt and frontcourt during the year. He had become an all-star in his first NBA season.

Most people involved with the game figured the Nuggets had a good shot at the title. There had to be pressure, since they were by far the best ABA team now in the NBA. San Antonio had made the playoffs by finishing third in its division with a 44-38 record. But the Spurs were eliminated in a preliminary round by the Boston Celtics. In another prelim, Portland whipped Chicago in two of three. So the Nuggets would be up against the Trail Blazers and their great center, Bill Walton.

The Blazers were a young and balanced team, one that relied on all five starters playing together plus the guys coming off the bench. In other words, it was a team concept with an emphasis on defense, the kind of combination that spells winning. Too many teams in the present-day NBA relied on one or two superstars, or a one-on-one approach, or a run-and-gun style without an emphasis on balance. Portland had a superstar in center Bill Walton. Walton knew he didn't have to score 40 points for his team to win, so he concentrated on rebounding, blocking shots, passing, and starting the fast break, much as Bill Russell used to do with the Celtics. And when he had to score, Walton was very capable.

The team also had a perfect combination at forward. Big Maurice Lucas, an ABA refugee at 6-9, was a perfect power forward, strong enough to rebound and muscle the big guys and good enough to score 20 a game. Bobby Gross at 6-6 was the small forward who did a nice job defensively against other small forwards. At guard Lionel Hollins, Dave Twardzik, Johnny Davis, and Larry Steele, as well as Herm Gilliam, were all fast and knew how to move the ball.

But why describe the Portland team when the focus is on David and the Nuggets? The Blazers were the perfect team to expose the weaknesses of the Nuggets. For one thing, neither Issel nor young Marvin Webster could cope with Walton in the middle. And Bobby Jones just isn't a real power forward despite his immense talents; he just doesn't have the strength. David, of course, was a superstar and would be on any team, but the Nuggets couldn't decide what to do with him during the playoff round with the Blazers. When he was up front, the Nugget backcourt suffered. When he moved back, the Blazer frontcourt really dominated. Of course, the Nuggets are a good basketball team and they played the Blazers to close scores. But they only managed to win two games, and the Blazers closed it out in six and moved on to the semifinals and, ultimately, the NBA championship.

David's game was obviously thrown off by the shuttling between back and frontcourts. He just doesn't normally string together games of 16, 17, 18 points. He did explode for 40 one night, but that was offset by Walton's 36 and Lucas' 27, and in that game Portland won, 110-106. None of the games were real runaways, but in the end the balance of the Blazers won out.

In the sixth game, for instance, a little-known rookie guard, Johnny Davis, came from nowhere to score 25 points, while fellow backcourtman Lionel Hollins had 21. The Denver guards just couldn't keep up with them at either end. David was at forward in that game. "Portland can beat anybody," said Coach Larry Brown with a prophetic air. But Brown could be proud of his team. In their first NBA season, they had done better than anyone had expected. There were just one or two flaws in their arsenal, and now Brown, Carl Scheer, and the players were aware of them. The team will undoubtedly make some moves to rectify the situation before the next season begins.

One thing is certain: the Nuggets got a piece of pure gold when they drafted David Thompson. David has proved to be just what everyone expected . . . and more. He is a consistent, yet spectacular player who has proven in just two pro years that he can play all-star basketball at two different positions. Not many players in the history of the game have done that. Perhaps John Havlicek is the only other player who can make that claim, and it took John a good number of years to reach that lofty position.

Yet through it all, David has maintained a cool head and the proper perspective. He admitted he was a little apprehensive when he came into the NBA. "I didn't know just what to expect," he said, "because the NBA had been built up as so superior. I was a little surprised at how rapidly I established myself."

He established himself, so well that some people began to say he had the potential to be the best ever. Again, David was candid. "Realistically, every player's goal is to be the greatest ever," he said. "Everyone thinks like that at one time or another. But only a few can truthfully ever reach that pinnacle. If I happen to be one of the best, fine. If not, I won't lose any sleep."

That's David Thompson, easygoing, honest, and, yet, a competitor. Perhaps his friend Monte Towe said it best when asked to describe David Thompson, superstar. "He's just himself," said Towe. "The same guy I met as a freshman at North Carolina State."

★ BOB LANIER ★

★ Professional basketball came to Fort Wayne, Indiana, many years ago. The town officially entered the infant National Basketball Association in 1948, but they played pro ball there long before that. Then, as the league grew and prospered, many teams in the so-called small towns with small arenas moved to big cities. Other just dropped out of the league to be replaced by new franchises.

Some of the teams that moved were Minneapolis to Los Angeles, Rochester to Cincinnati, Syracuse to Philadelphia, and Fort Wayne to Detroit. Owner Fred Zollner moved the Fort Wayne franchise to Detroit for the 1957-58 season. He had no way of knowing then, of course, that there was a nine-year-old boy running around the streets of Buffalo, New York, who would someday become the most dominant player in the history of the franchise.

His name was Bob Lanier, and when he was nine years old, the game of basketball was about as familiar to him as social security. "I had not even touched a basketball at that point in my life," Bob remembers, "Nor had I seen any more than a pickup game. Detroit, to me, was the place where they made cars." It would be another 13 years before Bob Lanier came to Detroit. And like many other players before and since, Bob wouldn't find Detroit an easy place to play basketball.

It took a while for many of the teams to catch on in their new home towns; Detroit was no exception. In order to gain the support of the fans, the new teams needed to be winners. Unfortunately, Detroit has been unable to produce a consistent winner. There have been a large turnover in players, several coaching changes, a great deal of dissension and turmoil, and few real stars.

There was also a notable lack of a big man. Well, Bob Lanier is a big man. He stands 6-11, weighs some 265 pounds, and has an incredible size 22 foot. When someone has such an imposing physical presence, a great deal is automatically expected of him. When Bob came out of St. Bonaventure University in 1970, Piston fans thought he'd be a savior, able to turn the franchise around single-handedly, much the same way people thought Kareem Abdul-Jabbar had done in Milwaukee.

What they didn't know was that Bob played his entire rookie year on virtually one leg, the other not at full strength after a knee operation. But sports fans often do not want to hear about those things. They tend to believe in the what-you-see-is-what-you-get philosophy. And what they saw was a big overweight center who didn't move well and was very inconsistent, especially at the defensive end. So they wrote the big guy off as another Piston failure.

It takes a long while to recoup from such a dismissal. And unlike Jabbar, at Milwaukee (who helped bring the Bucks from last place to a championship in two years), Lanier did not have the key players around him. In fact, Bob has played on a team that seems to be in a constant state of transition since 1970. And in that time his peers have acknowledged that he is perhaps among the two or three best all-around centers in the game. Still the Pistons have not been able to produce a big winner, a title contender, a championship-bound club. And that is a curse to all superstars.

Basketball fans throughout the country lamented for years that all-time greats Oscar Robertson and Jerry West never played on a title team, the one honor that eluded both veterans until late in their careers. Finally Robertson was traded from Cincinnati to Milwaukee where he helped Jabbar get that title for the Bucks. Without the Big O to provide backcourt leadership and stability, Jabbar would not have "single-handedly" turned the team into a champ.

It was the same with West. Despite the presence of Elgin Baylor in the same lineup, the Lakers kept getting close, but no cigar, losing in the final round on several occasions. It wasn't until the team acquired Wilt Chamberlain in the twilight of his career that they finally went all the way. Wilt gave them one big season and allowed West and the others to add the needed ingredients. One man cannot do it, and Lanier has never had those other one or two top players and a good bench to take his team all the way.

But in some respects it's amazing that Bob Lanier ever got to the NBA. Without his own drive and desire to improve, he might have been just another big guy out on the streets looking for work. Basketball did not come easy, and it didn't come early. He had to go out and get it for himself.

Bob Lanier was born on September 10, 1948, in Buffalo, New York. Like most other old, tired cities, Buffalo had its ghetto section, and that was where Bob's family lived. Bob grew like a weed. By the time he was 11 years old he had to wear a size 11 shoe. That was always Bob's biggest problem as a kid, getting shoes that would fit his always growing feet. "When your father picks up junk for a living," recalls Bob, "you don't understand about the comforts of life, like having shoes that fit."

So as a youngster, Bob thought everyone's feet must hurt. He was just happy to have shoes and never worried about a perfect fit. In fact, his feet were the first thing people noticed about him in those days. When he first tried out for a basketball team as a grammer school kid, the coach looked at his huge feet and told him that not only would he never be a basketball player, but that he'd never be an athlete at all.

That was not exactly the power of positive thinking, and such remarks could have finished Bob before he even got started. Even the other kids at the school often made jokes about Bob's large feet. One time his father had to go to school because Bob had picked up a classmate and had thrown the boy across the room for making a remark about his feet. When he was 12 years old Bob was already 6-2 and had size 17 feet. It couldn't have been easy for him to get around in those days. Most boys about that age go through an awkward stage, but imagine going through an awkward stage with size 17 feet! It wasn't easy.

During those early years, no one ever took Bob aside and tried to teach him anything about basketball or any other sport. He remembers that well. "When I was growing up there was no one to even introduce me to basketball. It wasn't until I went to a Boys Club in Buffalo that I was able to get started properly in fundamentals. I believe it's important for youngsters to have a good beginning. I hope kids today who want to play basketball don't have to wait as long as I did to get good instruction. That's why I've always tried to get involved with kids during the summers."

At the Boys Club in Buffalo Bob met a man who helped him turn his life around, Lonnie Alexander. He'll never forget Bob, either. "The first thing I noticed about Bob when he came to me was how tall he was for his age," says Lonnie Alexander. "He was only 11 then and I asked him if he played basketball. He said no! When I asked him why not, he said his elementary school coach told him he was too awkward to play anything. Well, the elementary school coach was only half blind. Bob had to be taught to run without falling. He was awkward, but not beyond help. I gave him a series of agility exercises to work on."

And Bob worked. Once he realized he was more than a walking stumbling block, he set his mind to improving himself. He kept getting bigger, but now he was also getting better and his confidence was growing too. He was becoming a good basketball player and was also a fine pitcher in the Police Athletic League. Bob also showed he had a good touch then by becoming a table-tennis champion.

Yet as big as he was, Bob wasn't an aggressive player at that time. He was so much bigger than the other boys that he felt it wouldn't be fair if he used his size and strength to push them around. Lonnie Alexander remembers this side of Bob, too. "I recall one game when we were playing the Humboldt YMCA for the championship. Their guys were just hitting Bob all night and pushing him around at will. And he wasn't doing anything to protect himself.... So I told him, 'You gotta get rough. You can't let yourself get mauled.' Then he went out there and knocked down a whole bunch of boys at one time. From then on, nobody took advantage of him."

Finally Bob made it to Bennett High School where he quickly became a standout. He was 6-6 and growing and played forward most of his high school career. He was what is now called a power forward, moving underneath and muscling out any guys who happened to be taller than he was. Despite his late beginning and his large size, Bob played an all-around game. He just didn't hang around underneath for the chippies. He was no longer awkward and uncoordinated. He could move well, though he wasn't overly fast. And he could shoot from the outside as well as move underneath. He was the star and captain of his team, the first time he had been thrust into a position of leadership.

Bob responded well to responsibility. He was a dedicated ballplayer and a good student at the same time. He led Bennett High School to a pair of city championships and in his senior year was named to the all-New-York-State team. Now he had to decide on a college.

Like most high school stars, especially the ones with the size, Bob had nearly 100 serious offers. But he didn't want to wander halfway across the country to some big-name basketball school. He decided to stay close to home and attend St. Bonaventure University in St. Bonaventure, New York. Though not a big-time basketball school like UCLA or Marquette, St. Bonaventure nevertheless plays a major college schedule, mainly against other teams in the East, but also some outside the region.

..After an outstanding freshman season, Bob reported to the varsity as a sophomore in 1967. He was nearly at his full height of 6-11. Naturally, he was now a center, and a good one. He was joining a strong St. Bonaventure quintet that featured some other fine ballplayers, including forward Bill Butler, who was to become the third best all-time Bonnie scorer when he graduated after the season ended. John Hayes, Jim Satalin, and Billy Kalbaugh were other first line starters.

From the outset the Bonnies rolled. Big Bob gave the team its final link—power in the middle—and they began rolling over their opponents. In the second game, against Gannon College, Bob popped in 33 points, Butler 32. Then in game five, against tough Duquesne, Bob had a season high of 39 as the team won its fifth straight.

By midseason the team was still unbeaten and moving into the national rankings. Bob was leading the team in scoring and rebounding, averaging around 26 or 27 points all the year. The club was beating teams from other parts of the country, teams such as Auburn, Seattle, Kent State, and Detroit. Plus they knocked off tough Eastern Schools such as Villanova and Providence. Many local writers began typing the praises of the big sophomore center. "Lanier is like a big cat stalking the middle," wrote one. "He moves in and out of the pivot with ease, and can score in close, or if given room, pop from the outside. He's already the best man we've ever had here and there's no telling how far he can take the club before he's through."

That wasn't all. Bob's coaches said he was "a pleasure to work with," and a "natural leader." He continued to be a fine student, aiming to get his degree. Interested in more than a fat contract from the pros, he majored in business administration, planning for a future with or without basketball.

But now basketball occupied center stage. The Bonnies kept rolling. When the regular season ended they had won 22 straight games, their final time out of the gate a 70-69 squeaker over Fairfield. Because of their record they were given a berth in the NCAA playoffs. In their first game they went up against Boston College. Bob was on, scoring a big 32 points and dominating the boards as the Bonnies won, 102-93. It was their 23rd straight victory and 25 over two seasons, an all-time school record. But their next game would be a difficult one. They'd be going into the regionals against an always powerful North Carolina team.

The Tar Heels proved too tough and too deep for the Bonnies, their pressing defense causing problems in the St. Bonaventure backcourt. North Carolina was successful in keeping the ball away from both Lanier and Butler, and they won easily, 91-72, eliminating the Bonnies from the tourney. Then in a consolation game the Bonnies lost again, this time to Columbia and Jim McMillian, 95-75. A great season ended on a sour note, but the team had still gone a lot further than most people thought they would.

It was a great year for Bob. He led the team in scoring with 656 points in 25 games for a 26.2 mark; that total point mark was a school record for a sophomore. He also grabbed 390 rebounds for a 15.6 mark, (another school record), and shot an incredible 58 percent from the floor. And to top that, he also found himself named to several all American squads—not the first team, but he was there nevertheless. The clumsy kid from Buffalo had entered the big time.

The only major loss the team suffered through graduation was Billy Butler, but it was a significant one. Butler averaged 22.8 points a game and was second in rebounding. Neither his scoring nor his board work was replaced, and, as the team opened the 1968-69 season, there was a lot of pressure on the broad shoulders of Bob Lanier.

The team started well again, winning four straight mainly on Bob's scoring and rebounding power. In one of those games played against Toledo, Bob had 40 points. But the next time out the club lost to Detroit University and three games later was beaten by Duquesne. They then lost to Oklahoma City, Villanova, and Providence. The club was 6-5 and struggling. Bob's scoring had even fallen off somewhat, and the word was that the pressure of having to do it all was getting to him.

But the club pulled itself together and rebounded. They had a big victory over Marquette in which Bob canned 36, a win against Niagara in which he scored 43, and then a triumph over Seton Hall in which the big guy set a school record with 51 points. He was again doing it all and taking his club as far as he possibly could. The Bonnies wound up with four straight wins to finish with a respectable 17-7 record. But it wasn't like the season before and there were no postseason tournaments this time around.

It was a very successful season for Bob. His shooting percentage was an impressive 58.6, and he also averaged 15.5 rebounds a game. His scoring average was up to 27.2 and was the eighth best in the country among players from major colleges. He was also named to the All-East team, and was also a second-team all-America selection of both the AP and UPI. He was picked as one of the top college performers for the upcoming season of 1969-70.

That year the Bonnies were stronger. They wanted to give Lanier more help and they got it for him. Moving into the starting lineup was Matt Gantt, a sophomore forward with great potential both in scoring and rebounding. Greg Gary was another new forward who would help. And Paul Hoffman moved into the backcourt to go along with senior Billy Kalbaugh. The club had a blend of experienced veterans and enthusiastic youngsters. And they had a superplayer in big Bob Lanier. The young players seemed to mature faster than anyone expected, and Bob was playing better than ever. The club romped through its first four games, including impressive wins over Detroit and Duquesne. Then they went into Madison Square Garden in New York to participate in the annual ECAC Holiday Festival Tournament.

In the first game, against New York University, it was a piece of cake, a 107-60 victory. Then came a tough St. Joseph's team, but St. Bonaventure ate them up, 96-61. More and more people were beginning to look at the Bonnies as a potential national power. The Festival final against Purdue would be a stern test. The Boilermakers were a Big Ten power and played excellent basketball. Nearly 15,500 fans jammed into the Garden to watch the final game.

Perhaps it was the excitement of playing at the Garden, but Bob was really sky-high for the game. From the opening tap he dominated at both ends of the court. He hit jumpers from the key and from the side, went low and tossed in short hook shots, grabbed offensive rebounds and put them back up, and swept the defensive board clear. The Boilermakers tried everything, but they couldn't stop him. And once the Bonnies got the lead, Bob showed the killer instinct and played even harder. When the game ended, St. Bonaventure had won the championship, 91-75, and Bob Lanier had scored 50 of the 91 points. He was named the Tourney's Most Valuable Player.

"There have been some great performances in the Holiday Festival," wrote one New York scribe, "but Bob Lanier's may have been the most dominant. He did everything a good big man is supposed to do. In fact, it's hard to imagine a better big man in the entire country this year."

After the tourney the team didn't let down, and neither did Bob. The club won its next five, and Bob had a 42-point performance in a win over Kent State. Then there was a setback, a tight, close, action-packed 64-62 loss to Villanova. The Bonnies just couldn't handle the Wildcat press. It was the club's first loss of the season.

But with Bob leading and continued good performances from Gantt, Gary, and the others, the club rebounded strongly. In the second half of the season there were impressive victories over Seton Hall, Providence, Canisius, and Niagara. The club did not lose again, finishing the regular season with a 22-1 record and a national ranking. That meant another trip to the NCAA championships. This time the Bonnies were really ready. In their first game they whipped Davidson, 85-72, and then took the measure of North Carolina State, 80-68. That brought them into the Eastern regional finals. They'd be facing Villanova, the only team to beat them all year. The winner of the game would be going into the finals at College Park, Maryland.

Many people were already looking past the Villanova game. The reason was that a Bonnie win would probably put them into a matchup with Jacksonville University, one of the top teams in the country. And more important, it would match Bob Lanier against Jacksonville's 7-2 Artis Gilmore, a player some thought was better than Bob. Most of the Eastern money, however, would be on Lanier.

But first things first. If the Bonnies weren't prepared, they'd be going home, because Villanova was tough. This time the Bonnies came to play, all out, all the way. Their guards moved the ball through the Villanova press with help from the forwards. Bob was moving very well and scoring freely, while he and Gantt controlled the backboards. Early in the second half the outcome seemed obvious. At the 10-minute mark St. Bonaventure led by 18 points and Bob had already scored 26. It looked like there'd be a Lanier-Gilmore matchup after all.

Then with 9:08 left there was a pileup. One player went down, then Bob went down, then Villanova's Chris Ford fell across Bob's legs. The players unstacked and at first seemed all right . . . all except Bob. He was limping badly. He tried to walk it off, but it got worse. The pain was excruciating. Two players had to help Bob off the court. The team pulled together and still won the game going away, 97-74. It was on to the final four. But now the question was, would Bob be with them?

Instead of celebrating the greatest victory in the school's history, everyone waited with long faces for word from the hospital. When it came it was bad news. Bob had sustained a very serious knee injury that would require immediate surgery. His college career was over and his future in basketball in serious doubt.

So the team went on to College Park without Bob and met mighty Jacksonville, in the semifinals. The Bonnies put up a tough fight. Gantt, at 6-6 moved into the center slot against the 7-2 Gilmore. Jacksonville also had seven-foot Pembrook Burrows in the lineup. And, while the Bonnies stayed in there all the way, the height of the Floridians was just too much: Jacksonville finally prevailed, 91-83. With the score that close, most observers figured the addition of Lanier would have made the difference.

But that's past history. UCLA beat Jacksonville for the title, and the Bonnies lost the consolation game, another close one, 79-73, to New Mexico State. Yet the 25-3 season was the greatest ever for the school, and had it not been for the freak injury to Bob, they might have gone on to the national title.

Bob was everybody's first-team all-American that year. He scored 757 points in 26 games for a 29.1 average and grabbed 416 rebounds for 16 per game. His three-year total of 2,067 points set a new school mark, breaking the record held by Tom Stith.

The injury, of course, was a crushing blow to Bob. All athletes fear knee surgery because of its uncertainty and the many weeks of tortuous exercise and pain that must be endured to build the knee up once again. Bob must have been down, because he even expressed surprise that he was named first team all-America. "The problem is with the media," he said. "They can make you or break you and there was next to no press up at St. Bonaventure. I was even surprised to make all-America. Maybe it was because of that good game I had at the Garden against Purdue. I really don't know."

The reason, of course, was that Bob had become an outstanding basketball player, one who had improved during each of his years at college. Bob was a worker and not a quitter. With the excuse of the knee injury, he could have easily forgotten the other reason he went to college, but he bore down on the books and got his degree with the rest of his classmates.

Then came the pro draft. Bob knew he'd get very good offers. After all, outstanding 6-11 basketball players are at a premium, rare jewels, players needed in order for a team to go all the way to a title. The Detroit Pistons were one of several teams that had their eye on Bob. But they had an advantage.

In 1969-70 they were last in the Eastern Division with a 31-51 record. They would have the second pick in the draft behind San Diego, last in the West. If San Diego bypassed Lanier, Detroit could take him. The Rockets went for a forward, Rudy Tomjanovich of Michigan. So the way was clear, the Pistons picked Bob Lanier.

The club needed him. They seemed to be going nowhere. They had one bona fide superstar in guard Dave Bing, but beyond that there were problems. The second best player was another guard, Jimmy Walker, but he didn't always work well with Bing. Walker seemed to be at his best when Bing was out of the lineup and he could run the show. There were also problems in the frontcourt. Otto Moore was a 6-11 center, but very thin and not overly tough on the boards. He was more or less a journeyman player. Otherwise the front line was very thin and lacked punch. The drafting of Lanier was perhaps the biggest cause for rejoicing in the team's history.

Bob was still on crutches when he began negotiating his contract with the Pistons. When he signed it he was still undergoing intensive therapy. So, in a sense, the Pistons were gambling. There's no telling how a knee is going to mend or how much mobility the stricken player will recover. And the Pistons took a big gamble: they signed Bob to a five-year contract worth some $1.5 million.

Bob came to the Pistons' training camp

still with a noticeable limp. It's odd that, no matter how big a name a man has, sometimes the old taunts follow him. Believe it or not, one Detroit newsman reported: "Bob Lanier's feet stepped off a plane Wednesday, followed a few minutes later by Bob Lanier." So here was a million-dollar player still getting ragged about his larger-than-life feet.

But that was the least of Bob's worries. He knew his knee was far from 100 percent. Yet at the same time he felt he had to try to play. He felt that it was expected of million-dollar players. In retrospect, Bob views the situation very simply. "I should not have stepped out onto a court until at least midseason. I wasn't ready." One problem was the knee. The other was his weight. During his period of inactivity he had ballooned up to nearly 285 pounds. He was pitifully out of shape, and with that weight it was even harder for the knee to bear up.

Bob worked as hard as he could. But it was obvious that his movements were restricted—obvious, that is, to people who knew basketball. To the average fan, Bob was just a slow, overweight giant with big feet. He began to hear things from the stands as he limped through the exhibition games. When the season opened he was splitting the center job with Otto Moore.

"Many of the fans thought I was a loafer," Bob says. "I remember hearing 'million-dollar bum' on a number of occasions and that stuff hurt. But in truth, I had no lateral movement at all that year, none in my legs whatsoever. I couldn't get off my hook shot and I couldn't move from side to side at all. I'm not a real good jumper, so I've got to move laterally to get into position to shoot and I couldn't do it."

As a result, Bob often found himself standing 20 feet from the basket, waiting for the ball to come to him so he could take a jump shot. He was also being moved around by other centers because he couldn't plant the knee and hold on. The whole thing wasn't working. One of his teammates even remarked: "Guys who are 6-11 and 285 pounds don't win games for you by hitting 20-foot jump shots."

The entire season was played on this note. The knee didn't get any worse, but it didn't get any better because of the constant wear and strain on it. Yet, strangely enough, with four new teams in the league and the NBA now broken down into four divisions, the Pistons had a winning record at 45-37. But they were in a strong division with Milwaukee, Chicago, and Phoenix, and they still brought up the rear in spite of their surprising record.

Bing had stayed healthy and had an outstanding season with a 27-point average. Walker chipped in with a 17.6 mark. Then came Bob. Despite the knee and playing little more then half a game, he managed to average 15.6 points a game and played in all 82 contests. Defensively he grabbed just 665 rebounds, below his usual par. Those who knew saw the potential; those who didn't figured he was an overpaid oaf.

So when Bob returned for the 1971-72 season he had a lot to prove. He was still heavy, about 275-280, but the knee was pretty much back to normal, though Bob later claimed it took a good two and one-half seasons before it was really right. "That's when I was able to do what I wanted," he said. "And it made a major difference in my mind."

With his lateral movement back, Bob was able to move better, especially on offense, where he had his hook shot again and was more accurate on his jumper. But some of the bad habits acquired in his rookie year remained. He tended to drift away from the hoop for his jumper and often found himself out of position for the heavy work underneath. He also had reverted to his old habits of not being aggressive enough, especially on defense. As one writer put it: "Lanier doesn't lean on people like Chamberlain does, and he doesn't elbow them á la Abdul-Jabbar. And unless he starts doing some of this the other guys will get the message and begin taking advantage of him, despite his size and strength.

To make matters worse, Bing was injured and out for almost half the year. The team was trying to work new players into the lineup and phase out some older ones. The result was a return to losing ways, only worse. When the smoke cleared the team was dead last in its division with a terrible 26-56 record. And they had the second poorest defensive record in the entire league.

The individual stats pointed to a good season for Bob. He scored 2,056 points in 80 games for a 25.7 average, making him the eighth best scorer in the league. He also hauled down 1,132 rebounds for a 14.2 average. On offense he showed he was all the Pistons had expected. But there's much more to playing an all-around game at center.

Two events that year really pointed up the strengths and weaknesses of Bob's game. The first was a gimmick, a one-on-one contest the NBA held to show as a half-time attraction on its Game of the Week telecast. Not all the big names entered, but many of them did; when it was all over, the winner was Bob Lanier.

Now Bob didn't win because he was bigger than the others. These guys are pros and most of them have all-around offense games. If a big guy isn't on his toes, the smaller man will run rings around him in one on one. So Bob did more than just back into the basket and throw in a lay-up. He shot jumpers and hooks, moved well, and played defense. He defended against guards, forwards, and other centers. The win was quite an achievement.

The second thing involved another great center, perhaps the all-time great, Bill Russell. The recently retired Russell was doing the color commentary on Game of the Week. Not one to pull any punches, Russell told it the way he saw it and in no uncertain terms. And every time big Russ covered a Detroit game, he blasted the team's defensive abilities and made a point of talking about Bob Lanier's defensive mistakes.

Piston owner Fred Zollner happened to be tuned in to some of the telecasts and heard Russell's critical comments. Instead of calling the network and complaining, Zollner did an unusual and wise thing. He contacted Russell and offered to pay him as a special instructor to help the club improve their defense. Since the price was right, the big guy accepted. Most people figured the move had just one purpose—to get Russell working with Lanier. Some players, especially today, would object to such a move, particularly after criticism on national television. But Bob took it well and still talks about it today.

"I remember how Bill greeted me," says Bob, usually with a laugh. "He said, 'You big overweight ox. I'm gonna run that baby fat off you.' And he wasn't kidding. It was run, run, run all the time. He had no mercy, but he just drove me the way he drove himself when he played. He had always been an idol of mine and I listened. Plus I lost 15 pounds, going from 280 to 265, which is a better playing weight for me. Bill also made me concentrate more. We also talked a lot about the game and that had to help." Russell tried to play down the whole thing. "I didn't teach Bob Lanier anything," he said. "I just tried to show him what it takes to win."

But as training camp opened for the 1972-73, it was a different Bob Lanier out on the court. He was using his weight more to bull his way closer to the basket. On defense he was clogging up the lane and blocking shots better. His rebounding was also more aggressive. In other words, he was becoming a more punishing rebounder, making other players think twice before contesting him for the ball.

The team showed a marked improvement during the season. Bing was healthy again, and the team had traded Walker, eliminating the incompatibility in the backcourt. Young Curtis Rowe from UCLA and tough Don Adams were both fine defensive forwards and also enabled the team to toughen up. The club didn't make the playoffs, but they finished at 40-42 and seemed to be a ball club on the rise.

Bob produced his finest all-around season yet. His scoring average was a steady 23.8; his rebounds were up to 1,205. His 260 assists placed him second to Bing, and his shooting percentage was up at 49 percent. Obviously, he was now playing a more complete game.

The next season was a hopeful one for the club. They finally seemed to have a set lineup with Bob, Curtis Rowe, Adams, Bing, and Chris Ford—the same Chris Ford who fell on top of Bob in the NCAA semifinals when Bob hurt his knee. Ford was now starting in the backcourt with Bing and doing a fine job. There had also been a coaching change the previous year with former Piston Ray Scott taking over from Earl Lloyd. Scott was now at the helm full time and was continuing to emphasize defense.

"I knew the way the team had been playing was not right," Scott said. "The Pistons had been the type of team that tried to win by outshooting the other guys, and that almost never works because shooting is the least predictable part of the game. We had to turn it around, take what the other team gave us on offense. Then we had to assert ourselves defensively and put the pressure on the other guys.

"It was a matter of getting my guys to execute these things properly. Last year I benched guys immediately when they didn't do what I wanted, and that included Lanier on several occasions. This year they're doing it."

The Pistons started winning. That surprised quite a few people, many of whom expected the team to fold. Scott had been right about one thing: defense was the key. The Pistons were among the top five defensive clubs all season long and it was paying off. And as the team kept winning, Bob Lanier found himself getting some recognition for the first time in his career. Coach Scott was one of the first to praise the big guy. "He's been our catalyst," said Scott. "He's what it's all about because he puts it all together in the middle. I'd say he's the premier big man in the NBA now, and that includes Jabbar. And he's still just scratching the surface of his potential."

Bob took a big step toward making more believers in mid-January at the league all-star game. He didn't start—Kareem did—but he came off the bench to spark the West team. Playing against Dave Cowens, Elvin Hayes, and Bob McAdoo, Bob was devastating. He hit on jumpers from the outside, then went in hooking underneath. Combining with an equally hot Spencer Haywood, Bob led the West to a 134-123 victory.

In just 26 minutes of action, Bob hit on 11 of 15 shots from the floor and two of two from the line for 24 points, almost a point a minute. He also collected 10 rebounds and was named the game's Most Valuable Player. All this on national television. For once, Bob got the exposure he deserved. "I've always said you need the media," he explained. "But there's something else. You have to lead your team to the championship to be accepted with the great ones. It happened quickly for Jabbar and Russell, but Chamberlain had a long wait."

So it was back to the hardwood. Once again the Pistons won. They seemed to be playing on a par with the other top teams in the league. And the more they won, the more reporters gathered around Bob Lanier with the questions they had never asked him his first three years. "I take Jabbar outside and try to drive the hoop more than I do against other teams," said Bob, happy to analyze his game after all this time. "That's something I couldn't do when I first came into the league. In fact, my second year he had a mental thing over me. He *knew* he could beat me. But he doesn't know that anymore. It's more of a heads-up thing now.

"As for Wilt, well, it took him two years to say 'Hi' to me. And that's all he said. I don't know what it was about Wilt, but I just lit a fire under him. The dude got mad at the sight of me. . . . It's funny but centers like Dennis Awtrey and Neal Walk are the toughest for me. Maybe it's because they push a lot and they get away with it."

Bob was still even-tempered, especially when compared with some of the other players. But Cleveland center Steve Patterson remembered one time when the big guy got mad. "We were playing in Detroit," said Patterson, "and I know I've got to really play him tight, heads-up, even though I'm aware of his great strength. Anyway, we're playing it pretty rough and suddenly—I don't know how he did it—I was leaning on him, hammering him, practically hanging on him, and he just wrapped his arms around me and threw me to the ground like I was a rag doll. It was like I wasn't even there.

"But Bob didn't even appear angry. As soon as he did it he looked at me, offered his hand, and helped me up. But he gave me a graphic illustration that, all right, you can play rough and you can play strong, but there is a line past which you cannot go." That's a line all the good ones must draw. Otherwise the lesser centers, who can't play you even-up on talent, will use you as a punching bag.

Bob continued to play the all-around game. One night against Seattle he scored 27 points, grabbed 19 rebounds, had five assists, blocked several shots, and even had three steals. When it was over, Bob said, "I've had quite a few games like this so far this year and I expect I'm going to have even more of them in the future. I want to be known as the best in my profession. I want to be respected as a player and as a man."

Yet, despite Bob's fine season, there were still newsmen and reporters who made a big deal about Bob's size 22 feet. Bob tried to look at it with some perspective. "Sure it bugs me the way a newscaster can say something about my feet and nothing about the talent I have," he said. "It would be okay if I was a clumsy ox. But I'm not. Maybe my feet have something to do with my ability. Actually I shouldn't really mind that much. It's made a lot of people notice me and I've gotten a good deal of publicity out of it."

Taking into consideration Bob's range and array of shots, it was now acknowledged that he was the most versatile offensive center in the league, combining both an inside and an outside shooting game. And now that he had conquered his habit of hanging around the perimeter looking for the jumper, he was much more effective.

As the season wound down, the Pistons found themselves battling the Bulls for the runner-up spot in the Midwest Division, behind Milwaukee. But with another new playoff setup, the team that finished third could still make the playoffs on the basis of their record. So the Pistons kept driving.

There was another aspect of Bob's 1973-74 play that should have changed many opinions, although average fans might not have been aware of it. They called Bob a loafer during his rookie year when he had the bad knee, not realizing that he shouldn't have been playing at all. He wasn't loafing; he was actually showing great courage. During 1973-74 he played in every game, though at one time or another he was suffering from a bad back, painfully sore elbow, badly bruised arm, a sprained ankle, a scratched eyeball, and extreme fatigue. But now there was no public complaint and no discernible drop in his performance.

Dave Bing credited Lanier with much of the team's success. "Bob took the pressure off the rest of us," said the veteran guard. "He did the things a good basketball team has to have done, and the rest of us were able to concentrate on our jobs."

That concentration led to a final 52-30 record, putting the Pistons two games behind the Bulls in their division and seven behind the Bucks. But it was a powerful division. Though third in the Midwest, the Pistons actually had the fourth best record in the league. Only the Boston Celtics in the Atlantic Division broke into the Bucks, Bulls, and Pistons monopoly. The other division winners, Washington and Los Angeles, had poorer marks than the Pistons.

Scott's emphasis on defense had really paid off. The Pistons were the fourth best defensive club in the league, allowing the opposition just 100.3 points a game. Bob finished with 1,822 points for a 22.5 average, 11th best in the league. He also grabbed 1,074 rebounds—a 13.3 norm—ninth best in the league. And his 247 blocked shots made him number four in the NBA in that category. And, as mentioned before, he did the little things that don't show up in the stats. This fact was reflected when he finished third in the MVP balloting behind Abdul-Jabbar and Bob McAdoo. But there were many who thought he should have won it.

There was still the matter of the playoffs. The Pistons were sky-high for the games, but would be playing the rough, tough Chicago Bulls, another fine defensive club. It promised to be a hard-fought series, with both teams refusing to give an inch at either end of the court.

The Pistons won the first game, 97-88, at Chicago, to take away the home court advantage. Things looked good. But the Bulls are scrappers, and they evened it at Detroit, then won at Chicago to take a 2-1 lead. The Pistons tied it again, but the Bulls won game five for a 3-2 advantage. Then Detroit won a clutch game, 92-88, to send it into a seventh game. It was played at Chicago and the outcome was in doubt until the final buzzer. But the Bulls managed to win it, 96-94, ending the Pistons' hopes for an NBA title. Bob played his usual steady game in his first playoff appearance. He averaged 26.3 points in seven games and grabbed 107 rebounds. And the club just missed going to the semifinals by a whisker.

But there was still cause for hope. Piston fans, as well as Coach Scott, Bob, and the other players, felt the team was on the upswing, that they would remain one of the top teams in the league. But it didn't quite work out that way.

For, while the club remained in the top four defensively, they suddenly found themselves next to the bottom in offense. And while defense is so important, there's got to be a balance. And, with the exception of Lanier and Bing, the other players couldn't put the ball in the basket with enough consistency. Bing was also now on the other side of 30 and had perhaps lost a step or two. And, despite a 19-point average, his shooting percentage was very low for a top scorer, as he was bothered by a formerly serious eye injury.

At any rate, the club played very little

better than .500 ball all season long, and when it ended, they were two games under at 40-42, right back where they started. Bob's 24.0 average didn't mean much, and he didn't even get 1,000 rebounds, stopping at 914. It must have been a disappointing year for all of them. They still made it into the playoffs, but this time had to begin with a two-of-three series against Seattle. It went three games, but the Sonics won it and eliminated the Pistons. It seemed as if the team was not at a crossroad.

Bob took the relapse in his usual fashion: disappointed, but not crushed. But one thing that seemed to be bothering him was the continued lack of recognition, of national publicity, and the omission of his name many times when the great centers were being discussed. "It's not the publicity I mind so much," Bob said at one point. "But if I played in a different city I would make more money outside of basketball. Everything is concentrated on the East or West Coasts. Players in New York or Los Angeles make more contacts with people who can help them when they get out of basketball. Remember, you're only in this game for a few years."

Because of this situation, Bob had to take the initiative. He used that same good head that earned him a business administration degree at St. Bonaventure. During the outstanding 1973-74 season he renegotiated his original contract to obtain a new five-year pact that extends through 1978-79. He also took the time to investigate and make some solid investments—said to include a shopping center in Florida, tax-free bonds, apartment buildings, and the stock market.

He continued to live in Detroit with his wife and children. And despite the Pistons' regression, Bob was still confident that he'd become a better player in the upcoming seasons. "So much is experience," he said. "You learn something every time you play a game. I remember picking up some things during a summer basketball camp I had with Dick Vitale and Jim Boyce, who are coaches at the University of Detroit. Anyway, it was just a little inside move I discovered, the placement of a foot to gain position when somebody fronts you. It will make it easier for the guys to get the ball to me in the post."

But the "guys" were changing. At the end of the 1974-75 season the Pistons traded Dave Bing to Washington for a speedy, assistminded guard named Kevin Porter. Second-year guard Eric Money seemed ready to blossom into a fine player. Rowe was still at one forward, and several other players were vying for the other spot. It was not really a set, stable situation, and the bench was weak. Suddenly the Pistons seemed right back where they started when Bob first joined them.

Sure enough, the season turned into an erratic one for the Pistons. Ray Scott was a casualty; he was replaced during the year by Herb Brown. Bob was hurt and limited to 64 games. His average dipped to 21.3 and his rebounds to 746. The team finished at 36-46, yet strangely enough were second in their division by only two games. Milwaukee won the division title with a 38-44 record. How things can change. Just a few short years before all the teams in the division had been over .500. Now they were all under.

The Pistons were in the playoffs again. This time they whipped Milwaukee two of three. Then they went up against the defending champion Golden State Warriors. The Pistons fought hard again, but lost in six games. Bob was back in top form in the playoffs, averaging 26.1 points and grabbing 114 rebounds in nine games. It was a shame Bob didn't have the help to take him further.

The 1976-77 season promised to be an interesting year for the NBA. There was an absorption of four ABA teams into the older league, and the rest of the ABA players were spread out among all the teams in a special draft. The Pistons came up with three fine players. They got 6-9 forward Marvin Barnes, 6-5 guard Ralph Simpson, and 6-6 forward M.L. Carr. In addition, they picked up highly touted, 6-10 center Leon Douglas and a 6-5 forward, Phil Sellers. They traded Curtis Rowe to the Celtics and dropped some of their fringe players. They now had potential for a fine team.

As the season got under way, much of the talk was about the new players. Simpson, for instance, had been a star in the ABA and at one time was called the next Oscar Robertson. Barnes was a player of vast potential who had shown brightly for a brief time with the old ABA Spirits of St. Louis. But he had the reputation of being a troublemaker and a divisive influence. He'd also had several scrapes with the law. Of the new players, only Carr moved into the starting lineup and played consistent basketball alongside Bob.

The backcourt was crowded, with Simpson, Ford, Porter, and Eric Money all vying for playing time; usually the two who were sitting were also sulking. It didn't take long for internal problems to overtake the team once again, though they were above .500, a team of great potential.

With all this happening, fans and writers again tended to ignore Bob Lanier. But some of the opposing coaches, sensing the big guy wasn't getting his due, were speaking out. "How do I rate him?" repeated Coach Bill Fitch of Cleveland. "I'd say he was one of the top two centers in the league, maybe behind Jabbar. But against us he's been number one all along. Some of the Detroit guys can try to go through customs with guns, but as long as they can get four guys on the court with Lanier they can win."

Golden State's Al Attles had similar thoughts. "I put him one, two or three," said Attles. "He's as good a center as there is and it looks like he's working harder this year. It looks as if he's putting it together. Whatever parts of his game were weak before, he's got together now ... There might be some centers in the league who do some things better, but when you're talking about the whole context of the game he's right there. And he seems to be the type of player now who spurs others on. He's just a different player than the one people are used to and that doesn't spell good news for anyone playing against him."

Before midseason the Pistons went up against the Portland Trail Blazers and their star center, Bill Walton. When the smoke cleared Bob had poured in 40 points and grabbed 13 rebounds. Walton managed just 14 points and 15 rebounds. That's the way Bob fared against many of the other top centers. Yet, when the fans voted for the midseason all-star game, Bob was running a distant fifth among Western Conference centers. And there was no way he could be that low.

Bob says those kinds of things only bother him when he stops to think about them, and he tries not to do that too often. But Bob also feels that his college knee injury and subsequent poor performance his rookie year put the mark on him. "It branded me for life," Bob says candidly, and his coach, Herb Brown, tends to agree. "Unfortunately," says Brown, "a lot of reputations in this league are formed your first or second year. The recognition for people who improve every year is grudging. And that's been the story of Bob Lanier, better every year. Right now his career is still on an uphill plane."

Bob realizes that his style often works against him. Unlike some the the thinner, quicker centers, Bob does not have those lightning kinds of movements. Sometimes he almost gives the impression of being a plodder. So Bob has had to learn to compensate in other ways. "I think the best thing that's happened to me over the course of six or seven years is getting the knack of helping defensively," Bob said. "I'm not gonna block a whole lot of shots. I know that because I'm not gifted with that kind of jumping ability. But I'll make people change their shots or block up lanes and hopefully we'll get more of a team kind of concept.

"You know, you come into the league with all kind of aspirations of just showing people that you can play. You're thinking about things like scoring or trying to get as many rebounds or whatever. You're trying to look at categories instead of overall things that it takes to win."

As the season progressed, the bickering among the Pistons persisted. In the frontcourt, Carr and Howard Porter were playing well, but Marvin Barnes, who was supposed to be a superstar, continued to have injuries and personal problems. In fact, he played a major part of the season facing a fail term for violation of probation, and his contribution was reduced to occasional flashes.

The backcourt was the major problem. Chris Ford did a steady job, but Kevin Porter, a most spectacular performer when right, sulked about playing time and said he couldn't get his rhythm going unless he was in there nearly full time. Simpson was also a disappointment. He didn't score as well as he had in the ABA, and his defense left something to be desired. Eric Money, supposed to have a world of potential, claimed he couldn't show it with the time he was getting. There were times when Porter, Simpson, and Money all asked to be traded.

This was all hard for Bob Lanier to take. He had been team captain since Bing was traded the season before, and he finally lashed out at his bickering teammates. "The situation is now at the point where guys from the first man to the 12th have to realize the situation isn't going to change just because we have a lot of talent on this club," he told the press. "As players we have to keep our thing together and not go off on each other. If Kevin starts then Ralph Simpson should pat him on the butt, but right now everybody's looking at it as an individual thing."

There was even a point during the season when Bob suggested he might leave the team if things didn't straighten out. But he's not the type to walk out on any situation. But then he took a vacation he didn't expect. Bob injured an arm and missed some 18 games during the second half of the year. In his absence, rookie Leon Douglas played well, but didn't supply Bob's offensive punch.

Bob returned toward the end of the year and helped the team finish in a tie for second in its division with a 44-38 record; at least the club was over .500 again. The playoffs didn't last long for Detroit. They had to go in a preliminary two of three against Golden State. Though Detroit won the first game, Golden State came on and took the next two. The Pistons were eliminated once again.

It was Bob's second straight season limited to 64 games by injury. He managed to average 25.3 points, but hauled down just 745 rebounds. There was no big scorer behind him. Carr and Howard Porter averaged 13 a game; Ford, 12; Simpson, 11; and Money, 10. It was pretty well split up.

But the fact remains that the Pistons were now a young team with a great deal of talent. Though he was in prison during the off-season, Marvin Barnes felt he had straightened himself out and was ready to show the world that he is a genuine superstar player. If he were to play up to his potential, he could take a great deal of scoring and rebounding pressure off Bob. And if Coach Brown could straighten out his backcourt problems (either through a trade or some sudden understanding among the players), the club would be strong and deep there as well.

So if the Pistons can pull together and the individual players can suppress their egos, Detroit may finally have a chance at that long elusive championship.

One thing is certain. There will be no problem at center. In Bob Lanier, Detroit has one of the major forces in the NBA today. But Bob is getting a bit anxious. He has said he would "be happy to finish my career here," explaining that his family likes it in Detroit and that's very basic to him. Bob also has talked about going elsewhere when his current contract runs out. "There are unquestionably some teams in the league that need some talent at center and will pay more money than I'm making now. I realize that. But I can't help feeling that something will happen that will cause me to stay here."

That something would be a contented team in the running for the NBA title. It's never been easy in Detroit. One writer was fond of pointing out that the great Al Kaline wasn't "discovered" by the national press and sports populace until the Tigers managed to win the World Series in 1968, some 15 years after Kaline first came to the majors and immediately won the batting title.

That's what could happen with Bob. But it's not so much the recognition he wants as the inner peace of knowing he's played his best and his teammates have done the same. That's about all any player could ask. But this is a very special player indeed. And there are now many people echoing the sentiments of Piston Coach Herb Brown. "Bob is the best player I've coached, the best I'll ever coach," said Brown. "And he's unquestionably the finest all-around center in the NBA."

★ DOUG COLLINS ★

★ In this day and age it would seem that a number one draft choice of the entire National Basketball Association would have it made: the big, no-cut contract, a wealth of publicity, instant elevation to the starting lineup, followed by a short road to stardom. Of course, it doesn't always happen that way. Sometimes the player simply can't adjust to the rigors of NBA play. Other times he may be eased into the lineup gradually. And still other times he may fall victim to the injury jinx.

For Doug Collins, the swift, all-star guard of the Philadelphia 76ers, being a number one draft choice was the beginning of a long nightmare. To begin with, Doug didn't want to play in Philly; he was led to believe the Chicago Bulls would draft him, keeping him in his home state of Illinois. Plus Phildelphia wasn't exactly a league power in 1973. The 76ers had just come off one of the worst seasons in NBA history, finishing with a 9-73 log. Who in his right mind would want to go there?

But Doug did go there, and moved into a rookie year in which he was beset by one injury after another, leading to personal frustration and opening him to criticism from outside sources who expected him to be a savior. Yet Doug hung in there. He stayed with the Sixers during a rebuilding period and slowly emerged as a star in his own right.

The rebuilding was fast because, like some owners in other sports, the man who runs the Sixers used a loose wallet to buy players and entice free agents to the City of Brotherly Love. But when the Sixers were finally ready to move on the NBA crown in 1976-77, they found there was no love lost among teammates. As has happened with many other star-studded ball clubs, the Sixers' play became a game of egos, rather than basketball.

Though often overshadowed by the likes of Julius Erving and George McGinnis (not to mention publicity generated by Lloyd Free and Darryl Dawkins), Doug Collins has shown basketball purists he is all the 76ers had hoped for when they drafted him: an outstanding guard of multiple talents whose main concern is making the Sixers into a team.

One of the league's tallest guards at slightly more than 6-6, the wiry, 180-pound Collins is also one of the quickest and most adept at moving without the ball. He had an extremely quick outside shot and often drives to the hoop in a hell-bent-for-leather style. He's capable of scoring big and in sudden bursts. He's also a tenacious defender and a cohesive force on a team beset by dissension.

But Doug Collins has worked hard to overcome obstacles all his life. He was born on

July 28, 1951, in Christopher, Illinois, and grew up in nearby Benton, a town of about 8,000 people. His parents, Mr. and Mrs. Paul Collins, never discouraged young Doug's early dreams of becoming a basketball star. "I'd play basketball by myself out in my backyard," says Doug. "You know, I'd pretend I was playing against Jerry West or someone like that. I'd do everything, including announce the games. My mom used to tell me she thought there was a backyard full of kids out there because I'd be making so much noise. And by the way, I never lost in those games."

One thing Doug objects to is the sometimes widespread story that he's one of these guys that came straight off the farm. Not that Doug has anything against farmers, but it simply isn't true. "Sure, I'm a small-town boy," he says, "but not a farm boy as has often been written. In fact, you put me on a farm and I'd be lost. I did grow up in a small-town atmosphere and enjoyed it. I knew everybody in Benton."

Doug kept playing sports and grew into a quick, wiry teenager. But competition at Benton High School was very tough. Basket ball was popular and the team was a powerhouse, compiling a 100-15 record during Doug's time there. So when Doug finally made the club as a 5-10 junior, he did not start. By the next year he was 6-2 and ready to assert himself under Coach Rich Herrin, whom Doug respects greatly. "My strongpoint is quickness," says Doug, "and I became that way by working hard at it, beginning in high school. Coach Herrin worked us hard in the off-season in track. We ran the high hurdles and the 440. He also had us run cross-country with weighted vests.

"In addition to that he tried to teach us good fundamentals. But in order to play you have to have quickness and we did so many quickness drills. So while I believe you are born with a certain amount of it, I think quickness can be acquired. For example, if you learn to react to certain situations you become quicker. If you think you can beat a man to a spot, you will, even though he might have more actual foot quickness. Basketball is a thinking man's game as well as a game of instincts, and these are things I began learning and working on in high school."

Doug was a still-growing senior at Benton High when he finally made the starting lineup. He began the year at 6-2, finished it at 6-3½; his shooting percentage was higher too. And his game continued to improve. Doug spearheaded the Benton attack and enabled the school to continue its winning tradition. He finished the season as Benton's leading scorer with a 24.8 average in 24 games. He also led the club with 115 steals, 110 assists, and 89 defensive rebounds from his guard position. He was named to the first team all-state squad, made the All-South Seven Conference team and won All-Southern Illinois honors.

The coach at Illinois State University in 1969 was Jim Collie, who left the university the next year to be replaced by Will Robinson. But before he left, Collie was instrumental in recruiting Doug Collins. Collie had also coached Doug's high school coach, Dick Herrin, at McKendree College. He saw a lot of Herrin the player in Doug and knew he wanted him. "Herrin was one of the most determined players I've ever coached," said Collie, "and it seems that he has imparted that trait to Doug Collins. Doug doesn't like to lose, and that's Herrin exactly."

After Doug led Benton High to the regional championship, he received scholarship offers from some 75 schools, including high-powered basketball schools like Vanderbilt and North Carolina State. Since Doug's high school career consisted of just one really good season and his natural personality wasn't one of cockiness, the thought of playing at a spotlight school like N.C. State was a bit too much for him. He wanted to stay close to home. So he chose Illinois State, located in a town aptly called Normal, Illinois. But ISU was no pushover school; the Redbirds played the likes of Purdue, Drake, Louisville, and other strong schools. Doug would have to work.

But the Redbirds knew they were getting a good player. Before leaving, Coach Collie said that Doug "has the potential to become a great guard at Illinois State. He has size, speed, quickness, ballhandling ability, shooting ability, determination—everything a player needs, and in great measure." So Doug entered Illinois State in 1969-70 and spent his first year on the freshman team, as well as cracking the books. Doug was an outstanding student in high school and continued that record at ISU, becoming one of the school's top student-athletes during his four years.

At any rate, no one worried about Doug's academic standing when he was on the court. He led the Redbird frosh to a 12-9 season, averaging 21 points a game. He was also the club's second-best rebounder, grabbing nearly 10 caroms a game. In addition he was up to his present height of a shade over 6-6, making him one of the country's tallest and quickest guards.

Doug joined the varsity the next season, 1970-71, and soon began making his presence felt. Feeling his way out he scored 15 in his debut, but in the second game against Central Michigan he really opened up. Doug popped home 14 of 32 shots from the floor and four of seven from the foul line for 32 points. He had taken charge of the Redbird offense and set a pattern that was to continue for three more years.

In the final game of his sophomore year Doug scored a high of 44 points to finish the year with a 28.6 average in 26 games. Doug was beginning to show the fans his speedy, all-out style of play. He also began exhibiting the unusual trait of actually running out of his sneakers, tearing them loose, usually on one of his determined drives to the basket. To some, Doug was too fast for his sneakers; his rapid acceleration just left the rubber behind.

At the same time Doug was becoming a court star, he was also maturing on another level. "I remember when I first came to ISU," said Doug. "I was shy, I mean really shy. I remember once when I hurt my foot I was too bashful to have the trainer change the tape on it. But Coach Robinson changed me without me even realizing it. Before I met him, I could never talk to people."

Will Robinson was a very special coach. Not only was he a fine basketball man who had devoted nearly half a century to coaching, but he took over the ISU job when he was 59 years of age. And if that wasn't enough of a long shot, Will Robinson was a black man who had spent 38 of his years coaching on the high school level. Because he was black he had been denied many opportunities to move up the the college ranks. When Illinois State hired him in 1970, Will Robinson became the first black man to hold a head basketball coaching job at a major university. He not only helped Doug develop his basketball talents, but also taught him how to deal better with all kinds of people in a world where intolerance and racial hatred are all too prevalent.

Doug came back better than ever as a junior, hoping to help the Redbirds improve their 16-10 mark of a year earlier. He showed he was ready for a big effort by canning 40 points in the season's opener, using his speed, quick jumper, and whirling drives. But the club had trouble finding a balance of offense and defense and played a little better than .500 ball the first months of the season. Yet Doug continued to be a devastating force with big games of 34, 39, 36, and 36 points. Then in midseason he popped home 55 against Ball State and followed it with 45 more against Winona State. Finally, toward the end of the season, the club began putting it together and winning.

In February the club had a big game against arch-rival Northern Illinois. In the stands was Pat Williams, then general manager of the NBA Chicago Bulls. William recalls vividly what he saw that night. "Over the course of a season, with scouts and your contacts, you end up seeing hundreds of players and many, many games," he said. "So if you see a player who makes your blood tingle, you remember it, because it happens so rarely . . . Doug had 33 points that night, and the club won, 86-85, on his shot at the end. When I left the building my body was alive. I was quivering. I knew I'd absolutely seen one of the great ones."

Other scouts were beginning to take notice, too. Doug was averaging nearly 33 points a game and was one of the top scorers in the nation. His speed combined with his height made him a pro prospect right away. And the reckless way he sometimes played showed the scouts they weren't dealing with a guy who was afraid to mix it up. He finished the year with a 32.6 scoring mark as the club compiled another 16-10 log. But they did it by winning their final seven games in a row.

After the season ended, Doug was involved in two dramas, one of which will live on in the memory of the participants and observers for many years to come, and both helping to show the innate character of the youngster.

The first involved Doug's future status. Would he remain a collegian or would the pros lure him away from ISU? In 1972 the ABA was still trying to survive against the older NBA; one way they were trying was to sign collegians before their class had graduated. The story came out that Doug had been taken by the Denver Rockets in a secret ABA draft. If he desired, he could leave school and sign.

Not to be outdone, Pat Williams of the Bulls also made a pitch for Doug. The NBA still wasn't signing undergrads unless their families needed money. Then they could apply for the NBA draft as "hardship" cases. A maneuver NBA teams used sometimes to go after talented undergrads. Pat Williams relates how it happened in Doug's case.

"We felt the Bob McAdoo was the only

really great prospect in the hardship draft that year and we tried to get Doug to come into it. Doug really hadn't had too much attention yet and we thought we could sneak him through until our pick came in the middle of the round.

"But you have to realize what kind of a kid Doug was then. He wouldn't go into the hardship draft because he didn't like the word 'hardship.' He said he didn't want his family to have the reputation of a hardship family. But, oh, how we wanted him." Of course, that is not to say that Doug's family was poverty stricken. Hardship was a loosely used term then, a way to compete with the ABA and get around the long-standing NBA policy of not signing collegians until their class graduated.

Doug quickly dismissed the ABA draft. He assured Coach Robinson that he'd be back for his senior year. "We've got some winning to do around here before I go anywhere else," he said. "I'll be around here next year for sure."

But there was one place Doug had to go. He wanted to represent his country in the upcoming 1972 Summer Olympic Games at Munich, West Germany. Since basketball had become an Olympic Sport years earlier, the United States had won the Gold Medal every single time. After all, it was an American sport, born and developed in the U.S.A. But in recent years, the popularity of the game had spread, and other countries began playing roundball with increasing regularity.

Though the Olympics are strictly for amateur athletes, many countries subsidize their amateur athletes, allowing them to practice their sports almost full time. In the U.S. most Olympic hopefuls must work out and practice on their own time, while working at a regular job to earn a living. The exceptions are college athletes, though they sometimes lose time from their studies to pursue Olympic gold. Some athletes make great personal sacrifices. If they win, they can then capitalize on their victories and cash in commercially. If they lose, they are soon forgotten.

Basketball has usually been an exception. The colleges resemble the minor leagues in baseball, preparing hoopsters for their pro careers. At Olympic time the best collegians usually make up a team that can easily run over any opposition, even though the so-called amateur teams from some other countries are made up of older, tougher men who are really pros in most senses of the word.

But the U.S. has really put together some great teams. In 1956 Bill Russell led the United States on to an easy gold. The 1960 team featured the likes of Oscar Robertson, Jerry West, Jerry Lucas, and Walt Bellamy, among others. That club probably could have come into the NBA intact and contended for a title the first year.

Soon after that, however, the big money

began coming into pro ball. And when the Olympic year rolled around, some of the top players hesitated about competing. After all, what was a gold medal compared to an NBA or ABA contract worth hundreds of thousands of dollars, or maybe more? Why risk it to be in the Olympics? After all, if a collegian went to the Olympics and, say, broke an ankle or tore up a knee, it was good-bye bonus.

In 1968, many of the top college stars stayed away from the Olympic team, and for the first time, some experts thought the U.S. might be taken. The Russians were getting better; the Cubans were good; the Yugoslavs were tough. Fortunately, the U.S. had picked a 6-8 youngster named Spencer Haywood, who was unknown at the time. Haywood dominated the backboards at both ends and led the U.S. to another gold medal. He has, of course, since become an all-star in both pro leagues.

In 1972 the U.S. team was strong, but perhaps left something to be desired; they were missing some of the big-name players. There were good college players on the team, men like Tom McMillen, Tom Henderson, Jim Brewer, and Dwight Jones. They were good, all right, but everyone acknowledged that there were better ones back home who declined to compete.

And then there was Doug Collins. Doug decided to play Olympic ball because he wanted to represent his country. And it wasn't long before veteran coach Hank Iba was glad to have him. Doug made the team easily and was soon in the starting lineup.

Doug and the rest of the American team will never forget their experience. They had a tough time putting it all together, and, though they kept winning, they were not rolling over their opponents the way previous U.S. teams had done. They just didn't have the all-around firepower and board strength. Plus, the other teams, with seasoned veterans (some of them in their second or even third Olympics), were getting stronger. That was especially true of the Russian team. They were a powerful, big club that also kept winning. Finally it came down to just one game: the Russians against the United States for the gold medal. The arena was packed to the rafters for the big game. But even before that big moment, Doug had some comments on the Games. "You have to remember they play international rules at the Olympics," he said, "and international ball is dirtier than the NBA. There are so many cheap shots every game.

"We worked hard and prepared. Coach Iba drilled us on defense for nearly five hours a day. When you have 12 guys on any U.S. Olympic team you're going to have some offensive punch. But Coach Iba had been there before and won it with defense. That's what he tried to do with us."

Some say Iba's defensive emphasis put a lid on the most effective U.S. weapon: a wide-open, free-lancing type of running offense, playground style. The European and Russian teams can rarely run with the U.S. but the conservative, defensive-oriented approach slowed the offense, so the game with the Russians stayed close all the way.

The Americans would get the lead, but they couldn't spurt, couldn't pull away. Sure enough, the Soviets would rally and close it up, sometimes with the help of some questionable calls, sometimes with tough play. "We couldn't get anything going that night against the Russians," Doug recalled. "And they were playing rough. I remember driving in to the basket, and a Russian player is right in front of me, crouched down, low-bridging me, and with a smile on his face. A move like that takes your legs out from under you when you're up in the air, helpless. It's stuff like that you never see in the NBA."

The game stayed dangerously close. Finally, in the closing seconds, the Russians scored and led, 49-48. Then with 30 seconds left they got the ball back again. There is a 30-second shot clock in international rules so if they could hold on to the ball, they'd run out the clock. Doug picks up the story. "They were trying to kill the clock, all right. The man I was on was at the top of the key. So I tried to lull them into thinking he was open, so I dropped off a little. Tom McMillen and Tom Henderson worked a double-team on the man with the ball in the corner. The guy threw the ball out and I got a piece of it and picked it up."

Doug raced downcourt and drove straight to the hoop. There were just three seconds left. He went up and was low-bridged once again. The ball didn't go in, but the whistle blew for a foul. Doug didn't hear it. He hit the floor and was momentarily unconscious. "All I can remember," says Doug, "is Kevin Joyce coming over and trying to relax me, saying, 'Come on, Doug, you've still got to shoot your free throws.' I was still groggy and I think that helped me, because I didn't feel some of the pressure."

So Doug Collins stepped to the line for the biggest pair of free throws of his life. It's accurate to say the eyes of the world were upon him, a far cry from the gymnasium at Normal, Illinois.

He took a deep breath and shot the first one. Swish! The game was tied. Doug stepped up again, bounced the ball several times, and took another breath. He tried to blot out the roar of the crowd. He shot. Swish! He had made the second. The Americans led, 50-49, with the same three seconds left. It looked as if it was all over.

What followed, however, was one of the most confusing and controversial moments in sports history, one that is still talked about to this day. "They told the Russians to bring the ball in after my second shot," says Doug. "So the guy brought it to the center line and I was on him. There was one second left and he was trying to push it up the floor when the ref stopped the clock.

"Supposedly, it was stopped because there were fans on the floor. We reviewed the film and it was the Russian team and coaches trying to get a time-out. Under international rules, if a coach gets off the bench, it's a technical." But no technical was called. And there was still time on the clock.

"They then took the ball in at midcourt and threw it off the backboard. We were jumping up and down, you know, we'd won the gold medal. Then some official from Great Britain came down out of the stands. It wasn't over, the whole confusing thing had to be replayed.

"So they put three seconds back on the clock and put the ball back at the other end under the Russian basket. The Russians were huddling with their coach, trying to get a play, but we were not allowed to huddle with Coach Iba."

"McMillen was on the guy who was going to throw it inbounds, really all over him. They made McMillen back off the guy. The guy then threw a long pass and the film shows he stepped over the line three feet in doing it.

"Anyway, Jimmy Forbes was downcourt in front of their star, Alexander Belov, and Kevin Joyce was behind him. Forbes jumped but the ball went over his hand. Belov caught it and turned, and Kevin fell to make it look like an offensive foul. Belov took one dribble and laid it in. They won 51-50 and we just couldn't believe it."

The United States appealed, claiming the Russians had been given three separate chances to inbound in those three seconds, but they lost the appeal and the gold medal. Although the game and Olympics brought Doug national attention, he was disillusioned with the whole thing, and still talks about it. "I was the most dejected person in the world after that, going from being so happy to being so depressed in such a short time. And you should have seen the others.

"Jim Brewer had gotten flipped in the first half and landed on his head. He had a concussion and was walking around saying, 'What happened? Who won?' Dwight Jones, they sent a hatchet man out to get him. He got in a fight with him the first minute of the second half and they threw Dwight out of the game. We played the whole second half with a makeshift team.

"But what makes the Olympics so tough is that we have college kids playing against men. When you're playing 31- or 32-year-old guys, it's tough. You're a young man playing against men. Playing in the Olympics is like coming into the NBA. You learn to grow up quick. Because if you don't, if you have a weakness, it will be expolited."

Because of the turmoil of the final seconds and what they thought was a complete raw deal from the officials, the Americans refused to accept the silver medal. But Doug has gotten over his disappointment and can look back at the Olympic experience with positive thoughts. "The Olympics gave me a great opportunity," he said, "playing against the big-name players, playing equally with them. It really helped my confidence. The way I feel now I'd like to have that silver medal as a momento."

When Doug returned to Illinois State for his senior year, many more people knew that there was an outstanding guard playing there. This time he'd be watched and observed; because of the Olympics, plus his tremendous ability, his value to the pros had jumped considerably.

During the 1972-73 season Doug became a bona fide all-America for the first time, making the first team in several postseason polls. But in some ways the season was disappointing. Coach Robinson didn't have the firepower to go along with Doug, and the team just couldn't seem to win on the road. At home they were almost unbeatable. But all together and it was a .500 team, no more.

It must have been frustrating for Doug, but he's a team player who sacrificed personal achievements his senior year to try to help the team win. Though he was third in the nation in scoring his junior year, he took relatively few shots, some 27 a game. And his senior year he was shooting even fewer, about 23 shots a game. His coach was hoping to get more players involved in the attack.

Doug's average was around 25 to 27 points all year long.

But in one midseason game against LSU-New Orleans, he broke loose. "I just made up my mind to put it on the floor and go that night," Doug said. "When you feel on, you just have to do it." He did it all right. When the game ended the Redbirds had a 103-98 victory, and Doug Collins had a career-high 57 points, an incredible performance.

Though he started out as a shy youngster, his years at Illinois State and his Olympic experience had brought Doug out. He got along especially well with the black players on the team, in fact, often used their speech patterns and expressions. Rich Whitlow, a black player who was a sophomore when Doug was a senior, recalls it very well. "Doug had the whole thing down," said Whitlow. "Blacks on campus were leery at first when he came on with 'Wha's happenin'?' and 'Hol' on, brother,' and 'Be smooth'—stuff like that. But he's genuine and true and he's learned more about black people in the last year than most whites learn in a lifetime."

On the court Doug was genuine, too. Unfortunately his senior year was somewhat of a disappointment. The team was 11-1 at home, but just 2-11 on the road, for an overall 13-12 mark. Doug's average was down to 26 points a game, but those watching him saw his total ability. He was a consensus first-team all-American and left behind a slew of records which still stand. His career scoring average at ISU was 29.1, as he totaled a record 2,240 points. His 57 points remained a one-game record until Robert "Bubbles" Hawkins, now with the NBA Nets, scored 58 in 1974.

Doug received a host of postseason awards, including one honor of which he was extremely proud. Besides being a first-team all-America hoop star, he was also a first-team Academic all-America, making him among the best student-athletes in the land. Now he awaited the upcoming pro draft, hoping the Chicago Bulls still had an active interest in him and would find a way to put him on their draft list.

But the wheels were turning in Chicago and Philadelphia. The Sixers, with their 9-73 record the previous year, had the first pick far and away. The Bulls still wanted Doug, but the only way they'd have a chance to get him was to trade for Philadelphia's first choice. So Pat Williams, Chicago's general manager (and ironically now the vice-president and general manager of the Sixers), offered Philadelphia center Clifford Ray and veteran guard Bob Weiss in exchange for the 76ers' top choice. The key man was Ray, a rugged 6-9 center, who the 76ers thought could help turn their team around. Ray was a defensive specialist and that's where Philly needed help.

The only problem was that Ray was coming off knee surgery and Philly wanted to be sure he was sound for the upcoming season. The weekend before the draft negotiations between the two teams were hot and heavy. The Sixers demanded to see Ray. The Bulls couldn't locate him. Cliff had flown to South Carolina to visit his family that weekend. He was finally located late Sunday night and told to get up to Philly as fast as he could.

As usual in those days, the Philly team was in chaos. Coach Kevin Loughery had just resigned to take the head job with the Nets, and assistant Jack MaMahon rushed into the breach for the draft. Then Ray arrived one hour before the draft was to begin. The Philly doctor looked at him quickly, deciding his knees weren't sound enough to take a chance on him. The doctor told McMahon what he found, and Jack called Philly officials quickly, telling them not to make the trade under any circumstances. "We were all set to sign Collins in Chicago that day," recalled Pat Williams. "But it was all contingent on Clifford. Then they called up and said he didn't pass their physical and the deal was off. I've never felt so crushed."

He wasn't the only one. When Doug learned he was the NBA's first pick, he should have been overjoyed. But he wasn't. The thought of going to the Sixers was disheartening. "I was very excited about the possibility of playing in Chicago," confessed Doug. "I went to school an hour from there. I had friends there. My attorney lived there.

I had never been East except for a short visit once.

"Plus Philadelphia had gone 9-73 and guard was their strongest position with Fred Carter and Freddie Boyd. Geographically, I wanted to go to Chicago."

That was to be the beginning of a series of disappointments for Doug and the Sixers that first year. Yet that draft was also the beginning of something new. Besides Doug, the 76ers also got the rights to George McGinnis in that 1973 draft, though big George was still in the ABA.

The basketball war was still on in 1973, and Doug was also drafted by the New York Nets of the ABA. So the Sixers had to pay to make sure he'd come their way, and the word was that Doug, like so many others at that time, became instantly rich. He signed a multi-year contract for a reported $1.4 million. But after that the bad news started. In fact, on the day of the draft, Doug's foot was in a cast.

"I was on a college all-star team that summer which was going to play the Russian team in a series of games," he said. Three days before we were going to begin practicing for that I was in a pickup game and I tore ligaments in my ankle. I was in a cast for three and a half weeks."

In May the cast came off, but the first week of June Doug had to have his tonsils out. Then on June 16, Doug got married to a girl he'd met a year and a half earlier.

Rookie camp was scheduled to begin on June 23. "On June 22, I was in a wedding for my best friend," recalls Doug about that hectic period. "The night before camp started I had to fly out of St. Louis to Philly. Well, there wasn't a hotel room to be had in the whole town. The place was absolutely packed because of a Cardinal-Cub baseball series. So I wound up sitting up all night in the airport there. I got to camp coming off torn ligaments, a tonsillectomy, being married, and with no sleep!"

Not only that, Doug was also coming to a town that had a very negative attitude toward its basketball team as well as its number one draft choices. The Sixers had had a history of blowing first choices— witness the names of Dana Lewis, Al Henry, Bud Ogden, Shaler Halimon, and Craig Raymond. They were all top Philly picks. And now Collins. He had the credentials, but many fans were skeptical about his Illinois State background. He'd have to prove himself on the court.

So Doug began working hard, as he had always done. He felt he was making good progress, adjusting to the pro game, and gaining the respect of his teammates. In August, the Sixers were playing an exhibition game against the Cleveland Cavaliers. Doug was guarding Austin Carr when he ran into a pick. "I planted my foot, and when I did, the foot cracked," said Doug.

Doug had sustained a stress fracture of the

left foot. Once again he was in a cast—this time for seven weeks—and he missed vital time. In fact, he missed all of training camp and didn't get the cast off until a week before the regular season began. Doug tried to get back in shape too fast. The left leg had atrophied, and he worked it so hard that he developed tendonitis. His highly anticipated rookie year hadn't yet begun, and it was already becoming a nightmare.

The tendonitis made Doug a limping, part-time player early in the season. He was just a shell of the daring, reckless, flashy guard he had been in college. He was playing less than 20 minutes a game and not even averaging 10 points. Cynics said he was just another first-round Philly bust. They had never seen the real Doug Collins and simply didn't realize how badly he was hurt.

In a way it was fortunate that Doug didn't have to suffer through the entire season like that. He played 25 games and in that 25th was guarding Austin Carr once again when Doug reinjured his left foot. This time he fractured the fifth metatarsal bone. Strangely enough, Carr once had the same injury, and when he saw Doug start limping, he said: "You've got what I had. You better have that seen to."

Doug had to undergo bone graft surgery. A small bone was taken from his hip and placed in the injured foot. Then he was back into a cast for the third time in less than a year—this one going from the foot to just below the knee. And it was really the first time Doug had been seriously injured.

"It was a very trying time for me," Doug admitted. "There was a lot of mental and physical anguish. I was home all the time, sitting around feeling sorry for myself. Injuries are a different world to an athlete. I had never been hurt in my life and now I had a rash of injuries my rookie year as a pro.

"People said to me, 'Well, you're still getting paid. What does it matter?' Well, that is no consolation whatsoever. I wanted to earn my keep. Any ahtlete who's been hurt would feel that way. But I guess the second injury, the broken foot, was really a blessing. I was able to get myself together mentally and physically and come to camp healthy the next year with an even start with everyone else."

But for a while the lost year gnawed at Doug. He had come to the NBA with such great expectation. Suddenly he found his rookie year limited to those 25 games, none of which saw him perform at full speed. He averaged just eight points a game and, since he couldn't move that well, made little contribution on defense.

Though the Sixers still finished last in their division, they really couldn't do any worse than 9-73. They actually improved to 25-57, but the personnel was still very weak. Veterans Fred Carter and Tom Van Arsdale were the leading scorers, but neither was an all-star performer. Forward Steve Mix was coming on and playing well. Otherwise the team was still made up of journeymen and a few unproven youngsters. Doug was in the latter category; he had proven very little, except perhaps that he was becoming injury prone.

When the 1974-75 season started, the team had made one major improvement. They resigned Billy Cunningham, the great all-pro forward who had jumped to the ABA several years before. Although he was over 30 and not quite the player he'd been in the past, Cunningham would surely contribute and help the young players. In training camp, Doug Collins seemed to be over his foot problems. He was moving well and playing with his old drive and verve. Before long he was penciled in as the starting guard along with Fred Carter.

Doug played well that year. He had some adjustments to make and was also coming off a season in which he had hardly played at all. So he had to learn about his teammates and about the NBA; in a sense, he was a rookie all over again. And taking that into consideration, he came on fast, keeping his scoring average around 18 a game all year, and every now and then exploding with a super game. In fact, he had the best game of any 76er that year, pouring in 39 points one night. He hadn't lost his ability to score fast and in bunches.

The fans of Philly began to cheer the tall,

slender youngster. His style of play made him an immediate favorite as they realized the Collins of a year earlier had been an injured player of extremely limited mobility. Knowledgeable fans also saw that Doug Collins was the kind of guard who was more effective off the ball. He was a scoring guard, not a playmaking guard, who preferred not to handle the ball, but rather to move without it and get himself free for a quick jumper or drive. And with his quickness and penchant for perpetual motion, he was very effective that way. When he had to handle the ball, some of his effectiveness was cut. But he worked fairly well with Carter, and the two guards had very productive seasons.

But it wasn't a winning team yet. In fact, it was essentially the same team as a year earlier, with the addition of Cunningham and Collins. The problem was up front. The club lacked a rebounding center, a power forward, and depth.

As a consequence they finished last in the Atlantic Division once again, although they improved, with a 34-48 record. It was a tough division, with Boston, Buffalo, and the Knicks all finishing ahead of them, though the once-powerful New Yorkers had slipped to a 40-42 mark.

Carter led the 76ers in scoring with a 21.9 mark that year. Cunningham followed at 19.5, then Doug with a 17.9. In addition, he led the club in steals with 108 and missed just a single game all year long. Coach Gene

Shue and others around the club were again predicting that Doug would be everything they had hoped for when they picked him.

The 1975-76 season was a year of change for the Sixers. The club was under new management, and the owner decided he wanted a winner: the best way to get one was to loosen the purse strings. The same year the Sixers drafted Doug they obtained the NBA rights to 6-8 forward George McGinnis, who was playing in the ABA. But McGinnis was unhappy and indicated that he wanted to come over to the older league. At first the Knicks offered a bundle of cash and big George signed, but the deal was negated by the Commissioner. Philly had the rights and would have first crack at signing him. The Sixers came up with a suitable, million-dollar, multi-year package, and McGinnis signed. The club now had its power forward, perhaps the best in basketball.

Also joining the team that year were a couple of high-flying rookies: guard Lloyd Free, who would leap with anyone and had a playground nickname of "All World," and Joe Bryant, a big forward with tremendous potential. The club also signed a player right out of high school, a huge center named Darryl Dawkins. He was a 6-11, 260-pounder with a world of potential, although the Sixers realized it would take several years for him to mature. They were building for the future and figured it was well worth the wait. In the meantime they had another youngster to play center, 6-9 Harvey Catchings. Catchings was not that rugged and a poor scorer, but he knew how to play defense and was fairly adept at blocking shots. The club hoped he could do the job well enough to combine with the other new players and get the Sixers into the win column for the year.

Things started well for the Sixers and for Doug. In fact, in the club's home opener, Doug drove so hard to the basket that he tore the sole loose from one of his sneakers. (Shades of the old Collins, all right.) Doug was producing. McGinnis was also doing everything expected of him. The club was winning.

After the first 15 games of the season, Doug was leading the club in scoring with a 22-point-per-game mark. And he was doing it with some incredibly accurate shooting. His 57 percent field goal accuracy was the best in the NBA in the early going. One writer went so far as to say he was going to be the next white superstar in pro ball. That made Doug angry. "I don't like to hear that kind of stuff," he snapped. "If a guy is playing a good game, that's all that's important. There's no use categorizing by race. Take a team. You don't break a team down. I want to be looked on by my peers as a good basketball player. I don't care if I get the spotlight if in my own mind I know I played well."

Doug also had a fan from way back. Pat Williams, the man who wanted him in Chicago, was not with the Sixers and couldn't be happier about the way things turned out. He said that Doug and Washington's Phil Chenier were the two best young guards in the league. "And for excitement you have to take Doug," continued Williams. "Chenier plays a more methodical, workmanlike game. But ask most of the coaches and general managers in the league and Doug's got to be at the top of the list. Selected on ability, potential, crowd appeal, enthusiasm, and team concept, I can't think of a player I'd realistically trade him for." McGinnis put it more simply. "I never saw a man as fast in my life."

Doug was also pleased with the way things were going for him and for the team. "I felt it was very important to come back this year in good shape. I played a lot of basketball, maybe four or five times a week during the summer. I ran a lot. And I knew with George and Billy, when they go to the bucket, there would be a lot of open shots for the guards. I wanted to get to where I'd hit them.

"I've been shooting well so far. I can tell by looking at my fingertips. I shoot right off the tips and I know I'm shooting well if the nail is cracked."

Like many athletes, Doug has his own way of getting ready for a game. First he goes into an almost trance-like state in front of his locker. He concentrates on the upcoming game and what he'll have to do against the particular opponent for that night. "I also have to get out of the gate fast," said Doug. "So I make it my business to run hard in warmups in order to loosen myself up properly. If I get off flying early in the game, I'm O.K. But if I start slow, I get to standing around. Pretty soon eight minutes becomes 12 and 12 becomes half-time. So before a game I sit there and think about who I'm playing, who's gonna be playing me. Then I go out on the court and try to get into an aggressive frame of mind."

Doug plays with an intensity that few bring to the game these days, and he readily admits it. "I play with lots of nervous energy," he says. "Some guys never show emotion, like Walt Frazier, for example, and they're effective. But I couldn't be that way. On game days when we're at home, I get so keyed up I have to do something. So I'll go down to the Jewish Community Center in Cherry Hill and run for a while, then shoot some fouls. If I sat around all day I'd get loggy and sluggish. This way I'm so keyed up that all I'll eat is a chef's salad before the game."

Doug was also feeling better about being in Philadelphia. "It's different going to a team that's down and being part of the building process. We're building a championship. We got Billy back. We got George. We got Steve Mix. We drafted people like Darryl Dawkins and Lloyd Free. Two years ago we were lucky to have 3,000 people in the Spectrum. Last week we had 15,000 there and they were all on the edge of their seats until the end of the game."

So Doug was coming out of his shell once more. He was becoming not only an integral part of his team, but of the community as well. He was a die-hard Phillies fan and in the summer often went to the ball park. He became close friends with the Phils' slugging third baseman, Mike Schmidt, and once even took infield practice at Schmidt's third-base position. "Greg Luzinski hit a rocket at me," he remembers. "I blinked and it was on me. It tore my glove off and you could see the laces of the ball on my hand. I could have been killed!"

That's because Doug is a basketball player. And he was showing it every time the Sixers played as the 1975-76 season got into full swing. Everyone was optimistic. Then, in the team's 20th game, disaster struck.

The Sixers were playing the Knicks in a close contest, with both clubs going all out. Cunningham got the ball and started driving hard down the left side. Suddenly, with no one on him, he let out a yell and crumbled to the court, writhing in pain. His left knee had given out. He was helped from the court. Doug Collins and his teammates didn't know it then, but they had just witnessed the end of one of the great pro basketball careers. Cunningham needed surgery and was through for the year. When he tried it again the next season he had lost too much. He had

had his share of bad luck, injuries, and pain. He decided to quit.

It's true Cunningham was not quite the ballplayer he had been in the past. In 20 games he was averaging just 13.7 points. But he was a veteran, a leader, a unifying force, an all-pro who had been there before. It was impossible to measure Cunningham's value to a young team. The club still had two outstanding forwards in McGinnis and Steve Mix, but without Cunningham they were missing valuable depth. His loss undoubtedly cost the team some games and some offensive punch.

Cunningham's loss also caused George McGinnis to begin doing more on offense. A powerful force both inside and out, McGinnis began playing all-pro ball. But some critics said he often held the ball too long, dribbled too much, went one-on-one, and left the others to stand around and watch him. It's a fact that Doug's game dropped off slightly after the Cunningham injury.

But it was also a fact that the Sixers were a much improved team. McGinnis, Collins, and Mix were a fine nucleus. Carter still contributed, and the younger players did their share in spots. The Sixers finished with a 46-36 record, tied with Buffalo for second place in their division. They were a winning team once again. And they were in the playoffs.

Unfortunately they didn't stay in long. That year the first round was a two of three against Buffalo. The Braves won the first in Philly, 95-89; at Buffalo, the Sixers came back to win big, 131-106. That gave them the home court advantage for the third and final game. But in a hard-fought, all-out game that finally went into overtime, the Braves won, 124-123. It was the end of the Sixers' season and a bitter defeat to take. But Coach Shue and his players were now confident. They felt they were a player or two away from a championship.

After coming into the NBA, McGinnis made first-team all-pro with a 23.0 average and 967 rebounds. Doug finally had come into his own, justifying the faith Pat Williams had in him all along. He averaged 20.8 points over the long season and was becoming one of the premier guards in the league.

Now to the matter of that extra player or two. Between the end of the 1975-76 season (in which the Boston Celtics again won the NBA crown) and the beginning of the 1976-77 season, there was a great upheaval in pro basketball. The ABA finally folded. The newer league just couldn't absorb any more losses at the gate, and with the bidding war for talent, players' salaries were sky-high. But there were some strong franchises and some outstanding players in the newer league. So the NBA decided to absorb four teams intact—the New York Nets, Denver Nuggets, San Antonio Spurs, and Indiana Pacers. The other ABA players were distributed among the teams in a special draft.

The Sixers had already covered themselves when they had signed ABA center Caldwell Jones to a contract two years earlier, they didn't expect to get him until 1977-78. But when the league folded he was allowed to go right to Philly. Jones was a thin 6-11, but had shown himself to be a good rebounder and shotblocker in the ABA and also had some good-scoring games. He could be the answer to their annual problem in the middle

They also acquired veteran guard Henry Bibby, who would eventually replace the aging Carter. Bibby was a small, quick guard at about 6-1, and Coach Shue hoped he'd become the playmaker to go with Collins. Bibby also liked to get the ball upcourt quickly, something else the team needed. Third guard Lloyd Free was an exciting player who could score quickly, but he was undisciplined and often thought he could do it all himself. But his potential was unlimited. There were a couple of rookies, of course, and a few holdovers.

That was how the Sixers came to training camp. With Jones and Bibby added to McGinnis, Collins, and Mix, and with Lloyd Free, a maturing Darryl Dawkins, Joe Bryant, Harvey Catchings, and the others, the Sixers and their fans figured they'd be in the running all the way. But no one expected what would happen next.

The exhibition season was in full swing; things were going well for the club. But much of the talk was not about the games; it was about a holdout player. And he wasn't an ordinary player. The New York Nets had him, and his name was Julius Erving, the famed Doctor J, perhaps the most exciting player in basketball. He felt that the Nets should renegotiate his contract. When the team refused, the Doctor stayed home, and soon the word was that he was available if the price was right. And that price would be out of sight.

But "Fitz" Dixon, the owner of the Sixers, saw stars in the sky. He imagined a trio of Erving, McGinnis, and Collins, and began negotiating with the Nets and with Erving's agent. As unbelievable as it seems, the deal was made a day before the regular season started. It cost the Sixers some $6 million to get him, part of it going to the Nets and part to the Doctor.

While many Philly fans figured the team was not home free with the two best forwards in basketball plus various other talents, some basketball people were cautious. Said one writer: "Let's not concede the championship to Philly yet. There have been other cases where superstars don't cut it together. And don't forget, this team has worked to build something all during camp and exhibition season. Suddenly the Doctor steps in, Steve Mix will undoubtedly sit down, and any team cohesion that might have arisen will now be disrupted. The Sixers may be in for more trouble than they bargained for." And that's just what happened. The team couldn't put it together. They were winning, but not as much as everyone thought they would. In fact, they were quite erratic, blown off the court several times by teams that should not have been carrying their sneakers.

To Erving's credit, he tried to ease himself into the 76er system. Not wanting to assert himself too much, he was content to wait for the ball, rather than getting it and taking charge as he had done with the Nets. But the club was often playing one-on-one ball rather than making it a team effort, and when they went sour, they did it big.

They were also having trouble at the center position. Jones was not doing the job they expected. Young Dawkins was strong as a bull, but still made mistakes befitting his age. They even turned back to Harvey Catchings at one point because he played defense and didn't worry about his points. Then he dislocated an elbow. The pressure was building.

Doug was playing good ball again, though his scoring average was down somewhat because of the scoring up front and the emergence of Lloyd Free as a shooting third guard. Then the injury jinx hit again. Doug sustained a severe groin pull that caused him to miss more than 20 games. "They even X-rayed it to see if the muscle had torn loose from the bone," Doug said. "I went through a couple of weeks where I couldn't even do anything. I just shot some free throws in practice. The blood from the tear seeped underneath one of the nerves in my leg. Sometimes, the leg would just feel completely dead, like it had gone to sleep."

With Doug out, Free moved into the starting lineup alongside Bibby, and things didn't improve. Many criticized the guards for not going inside enough, for pumping from way out when the two best forwards in basketball waited underneath. One broadcaster for a rival team spelled it out. "It's a strange thing," he said. "The 76ers have the two top forwards in basketball, yet neither one of them gets the ball enough. It's really ironic that you've got all that firepower up front, yet the Sixers are a guard-oriented team."

There were team meetings, complaints by the players, complaints by the fans that they weren't getting their money's worth because Julius Erving wasn't doing his magic act. Coach Shue wanted Doug back in the lineup, and finally began to ease him in.

So Doug came back as the third guard. He had to take it easy at first—no mad dashes to the hoop—but he was contributing. At midseason the Sixers were leading their division, but not doing as well as people had thought they would. Doug was named to the East All-Star Team, played 21 minutes, and got eight points. The MVP in the All-Star Game was Erving, who reverted to his old ways and scored 30 points. Some people figured he was ready to assume control of the Sixers in the second half. Doug was one of them. "A guy can't minimize his talents in order to maximize others," said Doug. "We must have Doc . . . lead. Then we must learn to follow."

Doug was one of the few Sixers playing real team ball. (One coach observed that he was the only man on the club to move well without the ball.) The other problems continued. Free, Mix, and Dawkins complained about the lack of playing time at one point or another. Erving was starting to assert himself more, but McGinnis wasn't playing as well. Some said George was already thinking about the next season and how he'd like to be with another team where he could be top gun again.

So to many, Doug Collins was playing the best all-around ball on the team. "I may be in the game 30 minutes and take 15 shots," said Doug. "But it doesn't look like it, because I'll get the ball down low or on the base line and shoot it as quick as I take the pass. A guy that backs in a lot, that dribbles around, then shoots, it looks like he's doing a lot more, taking a lot more shots than a guy like me." Doug's return had to help the club. Coach Al Attles of Golden State called Doug the unsung star of the Sixers, claiming that his "constant movement forces teammates to set picks, clear out, or do something besides stand around meditating on the floorboards."

The Sixers played a bit better in the second half. They had the firepower and finished with a fine 50-32 record, winning their division by six games over Boston. It surely wasn't a bad season. They had the same record as Denver and the second best mark to the Lakers, who were 53-29. So there was optimism on the eve of the playoffs. But it was Doug Collins who sounded a warning. "We talk of sacrifice and common goals," he said, "but when it comes time to do it, we stand around. When we need a big basket or key play, we fall apart. This team can't just push a talent button and get away with it. We're always going to be semi-disorganized. Yeah, I'm skeptical of how good we really are."

Doug played in 58 games in 1976-77. He was the third best scorer on the team with an 18.3 mark, but he shot 51.8 from the floor, the best percentage of his career. Erving finished with a 21.6 mark, and McGinnis was at 21.4. Free came after Doug with a 16.3. But, while the team still lacked consistency, their talent made them the favorites to win it all when the playoffs began.

Because of the new playoff setup, the Sixers drew a bye in the first round. They had to wait to play the winner of a Boston-San Antonio two-of-three contest. The winner was the Celtics, so the Sixers would be going against their old rivals in a best-of-seven series.

It was a classic series, an all-out battle of two titan teams. The Celts won the first game, 113-111; the Sixers took the next two.

The fourth game was a classic. Boston went up by 22 points and seemed on the way. But then Doug got hot and almost brought the Sixers back single-handedly. Showing no more effects from the midseason groin pull, Doug hit on a variety of jumpers and drives, constantly speeding past the bewildered Celtic defenders. Fortunately for Boston the veteran Celtics pulled themselves together and hung on to win, 124-119, to even the series.

But Doug had been amazing. He hit on 14 or 19 shots from the field and eight of nine from the line for 36 big points. At the same time he held his Boston counterpart, 6-6 Charley Scott, to just 14. And even though the Celts had won, Doug spoke with confidence and assurance. "I don't believe they are capable of playing any better," he said. "They thought they had us buried when they went up by 22, but we sure gave them something to think about by almost pulling that sucker out."

Then Doug added: "I'm really tired of hearing all that nonsense about Celtic pride and Celtic tradition. Those championships are nice. It's something I don't have, but a banner from ten years ago or last year isn't going to help win games for them right now. I like our talent against theirs any time."

In the pivotal fifth game the Sixers got it together once again. They jumped to a 30-20 first-quarter lead and made it 62-44 by half time. After that they cruised to a 110-91 win to go up by a 3-2 count. Doug was again the top scorer with 23 points, leading a balanced attack. After five games his playoff average was 24.8 points and he was hitting 57.3 percent from the floor. He was being called Philly's steadiest performer throughout the playoffs.

Game six was back in Boston and the Celtics refused to die. With Jo Jo White playing a brilliant game and scoring 40 points and veteran John Havlicek adding 25, the Celts tied it again with a 113-108 win. Once again it was Doug leading the Sixers, this time with 32, as one writer called him the Sixers' most valuable player under pressure. But now it was back to Philly for the seventh and deciding game.

To everyone's surprise it turned out to be a defensive battle—either that or the shooters were way off on both teams. Philly led just 24-19 at the quarter, and at half-time it was 50-45. The Sixers led all the way in the second half, though the Celtics never let them pull away. Both teams were cold from the floor and there were numerous turnovers. When it ended, the Sixers had come through with an 83-77 victory, helped largely by the 27 points scored by Lloyd Free, the only hot shooter on either team. Doug had his first off game with just 10, but it didn't matter. The Sixers were in the semifinals against the Houston Rockets.

The Rockets had a young team and had never been this far in the playoffs before.

They would not go down without a fight. They had shooters in Calvin Murphy, Rudy Tomjanovich, and Mike Newlin, and good board strength with Moses Malone, Kevin Kunnert, and Rudy T.

In game one young Darryl Dawkins played brilliantly at center for 25 minutes, while McGinnis, Erving, and Doug all scored more than 20 points as the Sixers jumped off, 128-117. Game two wasn't as high scoring, but Philly won again, 106-97, with Doug getting 20. Then the Sixers had an off night, and Houston got back with a 118-94 win. And in that game the Sixers lost Lloyd Free, who injured ribs in a collision with the Rockets' Mike Newlin. No one knew how long he'd be out.

In the pivotal fourth game Doug and the Doctor took charge. Doug shot 14 of 20 from the floor, and Julius added 11 or 20. The two finished with 36 and 29 respectively, as Philly took a 3-1 lead with a 107-95 victory. The Rockets managed to hang on with an exciting 118-115 win in game five, despite 37 by Julius and 26 by Doug. McGinnis was beginning to fall into a shooting slump that would carry over into the finals.

In the sixth game Philly closed it out, the Doc and Doug Show again providing the excitement. Erving had 34 points and Collins 27 as Philly won, 112-109. Everyone had expected Erving to take charge and come through in these big games, but Doug's performance had silenced any remaining critics.

There was little doubt now that he was one of the top all-around guards in the league. He had played brilliantly.

The NBA finals had Philadelphia going up against the Portland Trail Blazers, an expansion team that had built up and come to the finals in its first playoff appearance. The Blazers did it on teamwork, although they had a supercenter in UCLA grad Bill Walton and a great power forward in former ABA and Marquette star Maurice Lucas. Many called the series a matchup between team play and one-on-one play. Yet Philly was installed as the pre-series favorite.

In the opener at Philadelphia, the 76ers continued their pattern of the previous series: Doc and Doug did most of the damage as Philly won, 107-101. Julius had 33 and Collins 30 to spearhead the attack. Walton had 28 points and 20 rebounds for the Blazers, who served notice that it wouldn't be an easy series.

Game two was Philly's also, a 107-89 victory in which a brawl broke out between young Dawkins and Portland's Lucas. Dawkins threw a wild punch that missed Lucas, but hit innocent bystander Collins above the eye. Doug needed four stitches to close the accidental cut, but he was all right. And despite his wound, Doug had a game-high 27 points to lead his team once again.

The third game was out in Portland and suddenly things changed. The score stayed close until the final session when the Blazers suddenly opened up and ran over the Sixers, 129-107. They were back in it, and Philly was showing signs of cracking. Erving had 28 and Doug 21 in a losing effort.

It was the fourth game that really blasted the Sixers' morale. Portland humiliated them, 130-98, doing it mainly in the third quarter when they outscored the 76ers, 41-21. The balanced Portland attack and team concept were beating the Sixers, and everyone knew it. A tight defense built around the great shotblocking and rebounding of Walton was beginning to have its effect on the Philly free lancing offense. In addition, McGinnis couldn't seem to buy a basket and Free was still feeling the effects of his injury. Julius and Doug couldn't do it all.

Game five back in Philadelphia was crucial. If the home court advantage held, Philly would be all right. But it didn't. Once again the Blazers had a big third period, then held off a Philly charge in the fourth to win, 110-104, for a 3-2 advantage. Forwards Bobby Gross and Lucas had 25 and 20 points, while Walton swept the boards clear with 24 rebounds. Erving had 37 points and Doug 23, but it wasn't enough. As Coach Shue said: "It's very simple, gentlemen. We've been relying primarily on Doc and Doug for the bulk of our offense lately. So when one of them is off or they get little help, we're in serious trouble."

Back in Portland, the Blazers were primed for a championship. The first quarter was a

27-27 standoff, with the Sixers playing well and playing team ball for a change. McGinnis suddenly regained his shooting eye. In the second period, however, Portland began moving and grabbed a 65-55 half-time lead. Philly wouldn't quit. The Sixers stormed back, and cut a 12-point lead with six minutes left. It was four with less than two minutes left, and three with 51 seconds remaining. Then Lucas hit a free throw, but a hoop by McGinnis cut it to two.

In the closing seconds the Sixers had three chances to tie. First Julius missed a jumper, then Free missed one, and finally McGinnis missed. Then the buzzer sounded and Portland had won the title in a 109-107 squeaker. But they had taken four straight from a Sixer team that had folded when going up against a well-organized, disciplined, and patient team.

Doug also slumped near the end. He had just six points in the final game, but no one could fault him. He had played his heart out and the warning he had sounded about his own club, about their being "semi-disorganized," had come true. With all their talent, the Sixers had finished second best.

Perhaps changes were in the offing. There were rumors that McGinnis would go, that he and Erving were too much for the same team. Free had complained about lack of playing time and rumor had it, too, that his days as a Sixer were numbered.

But there were plusses. Doctor J was still

the greatest, and young Darryl Dawkins showed real promise. And then there was Doug Collins. Throughout the season and the playoffs, the stringbean guard proved a lot of things to a lot of people. In fact, all-pro forward Rick Berry of Golden State, who was doing television color commentary on the playoffs, noted that Doug "plays as well or better without the ball as any player in basketball."

He also said Doug shoots quickly, has a quick first step to the hoop, is an outstanding driver who can penetrate and spin to the basket. No one, however, doubted Doug's quickness. It was always there, the quickness, shooting, driving. And now he'd put it all together. The Sixers would regroup, and with their talent perhaps be back for another crack at the title. One thing was certain: the Seventy-Sixers' frontcourt would be built around Erving, and the backcourt around their 6-6½-inch whirlwind, Doug Collins.

★ STATISTICS ★

Bill Walton

Year	Team	Games	FGA	FGM	Pct.	FTA	FTM	Pct.	Reb.	Ast.	Pts.	Ave.
1974-75	Port.	35	345	177	.513	137	94	.686	441	167	448	12.8
1975-76	Port.	51	732	345	.471	228	133	.583	681	220	823	16.1
1976-77	Port.	65	930	491	.528	327	228	.697	934	245	1210	18.6
Totals		151	2007	1013	.505	692	455	.657	2056	632	2481	16.4

David Thompson

Year	Team	Games	FGA	FGM	Pct.	FTA	FTM	Pct.	Reb.	Ast.	Pts.	Ave.
1975-76	Den.	83	1567	807	.515	681	541	.794	525	308	2158	26.0
1976-77	Den.	82	1626	824	.507	623	477	.766	334	337	2125	25.9
Totals		165	3193	1631	.511	1304	1018	.781	859	645	4283	25.9

Bob Lanier

Year	Team	Games	FGA	FGM	Pct.	FTA	FTM	Pct.	Reb.	Ast.	Pts.	Ave.
1970-71	Det.	82	1108	504	.455	376	273	.726	665	146	1281	15.6
1971-72	Det.	80	1690	834	.493	505	388	.768	1132	248	2056	25.7
1972-73	Det.	81	1654	810	.490	397	307	.773	1205	260	1927	23.8
1973-74	Det.	81	1483	748	.504	409	326	.797	1074	343	1822	22.5
1974-75	Det.	76	1433	731	.510	450	361	.802	914	350	1823	24.0
1975-76	Det.	64	1017	541	.532	370	284	.768	746	217	1366	21.3
1976-77	Det.	64	1269	678	.534	318	260	.818	745	214	1616	25.3
Totals		528	9654	4846	.502	2825	2199	.778	6481	1778	11891	22.5

Doug Collins

Year	Team	Games	FGA	FGM	Pct.	FTA	FTM	Pct.	Reb.	Ast.	Pts.	Ave.
1973-74	Phila.	25	194	72	.371	72	55	.764	46	40	199	8.0
1974-75	Phila.	81	1150	561	.488	392	331	.844	315	213	1453	17.9
1975-76	Phila.	77	1196	614	.513	445	372	.836	307	191	1600	20.8
1976-77	Phila.	58	823	426	.518	250	210	.840	195	271	1062	18.3
Totals		241	3363	1673	.497	1159	968	.835	863	715	4314	17.9